A Century

Of

Baby Boomer Trivia

410 Memory-Boosting Questions For Seniors
From The 1940s, 50s, 60s, & 70s To Today -
Music, Sports, TV, History & More
(Retro Brain Games Quiz Book)

By

Garrett Monroe

Table Of Contents

Your Nostalgic Fun Pack

As a way of saying thank you for your purchase, we're giving you our "Nostalgic Fun pack": four FREE downloads that are exclusive to our book readers!

Here's what you'll get:

1. Boomer Brain Teasers: 75 Trivia Questions Spanning the '60s, '70s, '80s, and '90s

2. The Golden Years Word Find: 20 Nostalgic Word Searches

3. Heartwarming Tales: 20 Uplifting Short Stories for Seniors

4. Retirement Movie Marathon: 20 Feel-Good Movies For Seniors

To download your bonuses, you can go to MonroeMethod.com/trivia-bonus or scan the QR code below:

Get Ready For A Trivia Adventure!

Remember the good old days when music had real soul, TV shows were must-see events, and every trip to the movies was an experience? Well, you're in for a treat. This trivia book is your ticket back to those unforgettable moments, specifically designed for seniors and baby boomers who know the true meaning of the good times.

We've packed this book with 410 carefully crafted trivia questions that will take you on a delightful journey through the best of the last century, from the 1940s to today. Whether you're a rock 'n' roll aficionado, a TV buff, or someone who can still recall the thrill of witnessing history in the making, there's something here for everyone.

Each question in this book is multiple-choice, making it easy and fun to dive into. And don't worry—there's no need to keep track of your answers in your head. At the end of each decade chapter, you'll find an easy-to-reference answer key to see how well you did!

Why trivia, you ask? Well, it's more than just fun—it's a way to keep your mind sharp, relive the highlights of the past, and maybe even impress your friends with your unbeatable knowledge of everything from classic sports moments to iconic movie lines.

So, are you ready to test your knowledge, relive the greatest hits of your life, and maybe even learn a thing or two along the way? Grab your reading glasses, get comfortable, and dive into the ultimate trivia challenge.

1940s Questions

#1 - WHAT YEAR DID WORLD WAR II END?

A) 1945   C) 1949

B) 1914   D) 1944

#2 - WHO WAS THE FIRST AND ONLY US PRESIDENT TO SERVE A
THIRD TERM?

A) Franklin D. Roosevelt   C) Richard Nixon

B) Harry S. Truman   D) Calvin Coolidge

#3 - WHEN DID THE D-DAY NORMANDY LANDINGS OCCUR?

A) November 8, 1942

C) April 11, 1941

B) January 12, 1945

D) June 6, 1944

#4 - WHAT YEAR WAS THE NATIONAL BASKETBALL ASSOCIATION (NBA) FORMED?

A) 1945

C) 1946

B) 1949

D) 1944

#5 - WHAT IS THE NAME OF WALT DISNEY'S SECOND FEATURE-LENGTH MOVIE THAT WAS RELEASED IN 1940?

A) Pinocchio

C) Snow White

B) Cinderella

D) Bambi

#6 - WHAT WAS THE CAUSE OF FRANKLIN D. ROOSEVELT'S DEATH?

A) Lung cancer

C) Alzheimer's disease

B) Cerebral hemorrhage

D) Pneumonia

#7 - HOW MANY JACKS DOES A PLAYER USE IN THE FAMOUS 1940S GAME OF "JACKS"?

A) 2

C) 1

B) 4

D) 5

#8 - WHICH OF THE FOLLOWING WAS ONE OF THE ICONIC JUKEBOX MODELS IN THE 1940S?

A) LG

C) Sony

B) Samsung

D) Wurlitzer 1015 model

#9 - WHAT BAND COMPOSED THE SONG "TAKE THE 'A' TRAIN"?

A) Duke Ellington Orchestra

C) Count Basie Orchestra

B) Glenn Miller Orchestra

D) The Four Tunes

#10 - WHICH ICONIC US LANDMARK WAS COMPLETED ON OCTOBER 31, 1941?

A) Mount Rushmore National Memorial

C) Golden Gate Bridge

D) Space Needle

B) Crazy Horse Memorial

#11 - WHAT YEAR WAS THE MICROWAVE OVEN INVENTED?

A) 1944

C) 1945

B) 1946

D) 1947

#12 - WHAT YEAR DID THE MANUFACTURE OF VEHICLES FOR THE CIVILIAN MARKET TEMPORARILY CEASE IN THE U.S.?

A) 1939

C) 1945

B) 1942

D) 1944

#13 - WHICH 1940S FASHION STYLE BECAME A SYMBOL OF PATRIOTISM DURING THE WAR YEARS?

A) The New Look

C) Utility Clothing

B) Victory Suit

D) Shirt Dress

#14 - HOW MANY OSCARS DID THE MOVIE *GONE WITH THE WIND* WIN DURING THE 12TH ACADEMY AWARDS IN 1940?

A) 2

C) 5

B) 8

D) 3

#15 - WHICH CITY WAS ORIGINALLY SCHEDULED TO HOST THE 1944 SUMMER OLYMPICS BEFORE IT WAS CANCELED?

A) Berlin

C) New York

B) Texas

D) London

#16 - WHICH BASEBALL PLAYER WAS SUSPENDED FROM EBBETS FIELD FOR "INCITING A RIOT"?

A) Leo Durocher

C) Rudy York

B) Ted Williams

D) Bob Elliott

#17 - HOW MANY WORLD SERIES MATCH-UPS DID NEW YORK YANKEES PLAY FROM 1940 to 1949?

A) 1

C) 4

B) 3

D) 5

#18 - WHAT IS THE NAME OF THE WOMEN'S BRANCH OF THE U.S. ARMY THAT WAS FORMED IN 1942 TO BRING OPPORTUNITIES AND EQUALITY TO WOMEN WHO SERVED IN THE AMERICAN MILITARY?

A) Women Accepted for Volunteer Emergency Service

B) Army Nurse Corps

C) Women's Army Auxiliary Corps

D) Marine Corps Women's Reserve

#19 - WHAT WAS THE NICKNAME OF THE FIRST FORD CAR DESIGNED AND BUILT WITHOUT HENRY FORD'S OVERSIGHT?

A) Shoebox

B) Quadricycle

C) Tin Lizzie

D) Rust Bucket

#20 - *THE GRAPES OF WRATH* IS AN ICONIC MOVIE BASED ON A NOVEL WRITTEN BY WHICH AUTHOR?

A) John Steinbeck

B) Daphne du Maurier

C) Philip Barry

D) Betty Smith

#21 - WHICH NFL TEAM SIGNED KENNY WASHINGTON IN 1946, ENDING THE LEAGUE'S 12-YEAR BAN ON BLACK PLAYERS?

A) New York Giants

B) Arizona Cardinals

C) Chicago Bears

D) Los Angeles Rams

#22 - WHO ACCIDENTALLY INVENTED THE SLINKY TOY IN 1943?

A) James Gilbert E. Wright   C) Richard T. James

B) Ernő Rubik   D) Abe Book

#23 - FROM WHICH STATE DID THE FIRST NONSTOP FLIGHT AROUND THE WORLD TAKE OFF?

A) Arizona   C) Florida

B) Ohio   D) Texas

#24 - WHICH ACTOR APPEARED AT THE COURTHOUSE IN 1944 AFTER BEING ARRESTED FOR VIOLATING THE MANN ACT OF 1909?

A) Humphrey Bogart   C) Chuck Berry

B) Charlie Chaplin   D) James Stewart

#25 - WHEN DID THE FAMOUS MOVIE *CASABLANCA* FIRST PREMIERE?

A) November 26, 1942   C) January 23, 1943

B) May 3, 1941   D) January 11, 1940

#26 - WHICH AMERICAN MUSICIAN WENT MISSING WHILE ON HIS WAY TO PERFORM FOR TROOPS IN PARIS ON CHRISTMAS DAY 1944?

A) Frank Sinatra   C) Bing Crosby

B) Louis Armstrong   D) Glenn Miller

#27 - WHICH 1940S DANCE WAS INVENTED BY DANCER HARLEM?

A) Lindy Hop

C) Rock and Roll

B) Jive

D) Charleston

#28 - HOW MANY COUNTS ARE IN THE BASIC STEP OF EAST COAST SWING?

A) 3

C) 7

B) 8

D) 6

#29 - WHICH FASHION LOOK BECAME FAMOUS DUE TO THE HARSH ECONOMIC CLIMATE DURING WARTIME?

A) New Look

C) Retro House Dress

B) Utility Clothing

D) Shirt Dress

#30 - WHAT YEAR WAS THE AMERICAN ACADEMY OF DENTAL MEDICINE FOUNDED?

A) 1940

C) 1945

B) 1949

D) 1944

1940s: Answer Key

ANSWER #1: A) 1945

After atomic bombs were dropped on Hiroshima and Nagasaki, Japan surrendered in September 1945, following Germany's surrender on May 8. These events were crucial in ending World War II.

ANSWER #2: A) FRANKLIN D. ROOSEVELT

The third election occurred as World War II began and during the Great Depression, helping Roosevelt argue for stability. Two years after his death, Congress passed an amendment limiting presidents to two terms.

ANSWER #3: D) JUNE 6, 1944

The D-Day Normandy operations, codenamed OVERLORD, saw 133,000 troops land on the beaches, with 10,300 Allied soldiers losing their lives. By June's end, around 850,000 troops had arrived to liberate France.

ANSWER #4: B) 1949

On August 3, 1949, the National Basketball League and the Basketball Association of America merged to create the NBA, ending a three-year rivalry. The NBA has grown into one of the world's top sports leagues.

ANSWER #5: A) PINOCCHIO

Released on February 23, 1940, *Pinocchio* became an animated classic, winning two Academy Awards for Best Original Score and Song. It was adapted from Carlo Lorenzini's 1883 novel *The Adventures of Pinocchio*.

ANSWER #6: B) CEREBRAL HEMORRHAGE

On April 12, 1945, President Roosevelt collapsed and died while sitting for a portrait. His health had been in decline, suffering from ailments like bronchitis and high blood pressure.

ANSWER #7: D) 5

The game generally requires the player to throw five jacks in the air and catch them on the back of the hand before the ball bounces. The jacks can be made of metal, pieces of bone, clay, or small stones.

Answer #8: D) WURLITZER 1015 MODEL

The 1940s marked the golden age of jukeboxes, where people inserted coins to play songs in bars. The Wurlitzer 1015, known as the Bubbler, featured bubble-filled tubes along its arched top.

ANSWER #9: A) DUKE ELLINGTON ORCHESTRA

"Take the 'A' Train," written by Billy Strayhorn, became a signature piece for Duke Ellington's orchestra and brought them significant success. In 1976, it was inducted into the Grammy Hall of Fame.

ANSWER #10: A) MOUNT RUSHMORE NATIONAL MEMORIAL

Mount Rushmore, honoring Presidents Washington, Jefferson, Roosevelt, and Lincoln, began in 1927 but faced delays **due to various** challenges. It was declared complete on October 31, 1941, when funds ran out.

ANSWER #11: B) 1946

Percy Spencer filed the first microwave oven patent in 1945. Initially focused on developing magnetrons for WWII, Spencer accidentally discovered its food-heating ability and began experiments that led to the microwave oven.

ANSWER #12: B) 1942

Automobile production shifted to war efforts, with civilian car and truck manufacturing banned from February 1942 to October 1945. The industry was retooled to produce jeeps, trucks, airplanes, bombs, helmets, and torpedoes.

Answer #13: B) Victory Suit

The Victory Suit, a 1940s symbol of women's empowerment and patriotism, featured below-the-knee skirts and boxy jackets with padded shoulders and fabric fastenings instead of buttons. It was both practical and stylish.

ANSWER #14: B) 8

Gone with the Wind follows manipulative Southern belle Scarlett O'Hara as she falls for a charming gentleman during the Civil War. The film won multiple Academy Awards, including Best Picture **and** Best Actress.

ANSWER #15: D) LONDON

The 1940 Summer Olympics in London and Winter Olympics in Italy were canceled due to the war. London later hosted the 1948 Summer Games, though Japanese and German athletes were banned from participating.

ANSWER #16: A) LEO DUROCHER

The incident occurred when a fan attacked an umpire on the field after a game between the Cincinnati Reds and the Dodgers. In 1947, Leo Durocher was also suspended for a year by Commissioner Happy Chandler due to gambling.

ANSWER #17: D) 5

In the 1940s, the New York Yankees reached the World Series five times

(1941, 1942, 1943, 1947, 1949), winning four. They also began a streak of five consecutive titles from 1949 to 1953, with a record of 929-609 in the decade.

ANSWER #18: C) WOMEN'S ARMY AUXILIARY CORPS

U.S. Representative Edith Nourse Rogers of Massachusetts, inspired by women's roles in World War I, introduced a bill to create the Women's Army Auxiliary Corps (WAAC).

ANSWER #19: A) SHOEBOX

After Henry Ford's death in 1947, Ford introduced the 1949 model, which marked a major shift in car design. Over 1.1 million units were built, and the "Shoebox" ranged in price from $1,333 to $2,264.

ANSWER #20: A) JOHN STEINBECK

The Grapes of Wrath portrays the hardships of migrant farmworkers during the Great Depression. Steinbeck sold the rights, and the film adaptation is praised for its accurate depiction of historical and social issues.

ANSWER #21: D) LOS ANGELES RAMS

NFL owners secretly banned Black players in 1933. Facing the possibility of losing their lease on the Los Angeles Coliseum, the Los Angeles Rams signed Kenny Washington in 1946, breaking the 12-year ban on Black players.

ANSWER #22: C) RICHARD T. JAMES

Richard James was developing a device to stabilize equipment during sea transport when he accidentally knocked it off a shelf and noticed it "walked down" on its own. He and his wife, Betty, turned this discovery into a successful toy business.

ANSWER #23: D) TEXAS

On February 26, 1949, Lucky Lady II, a plane with a 14-man crew, took off from a Texas military base. After flying nearly 38,000 kilometers over 94 hours, it returned on March 2. The mission was kept secret.

ANSWER #24: B) CHARLIE CHAPLIN

The Mann Act criminalized the transportation of women across state lines. Charlie Chaplin was charged with transporting a woman for immoral purposes, although he was eventually cleared of the charges.

ANSWER #25: A) NOVEMBER 26, 1942

Casablanca is one of the most famous films of all time. Due to real-world events, the release of the movie was expedited. It was originally scheduled for early 1943 but premiered on November 26, 1942.

ANSWER #26: D) GLENN MILLER

Glenn Miller, a leading figure in the 1930s and 1940s with hits like "In the Mood" and "Moonlight Serenade," vanished when his plane disappeared over the English Channel. His disappearance remains an unsolved mystery.

ANSWER #27: A) LINDY HOP

The Lindy Hop, created in 1927 by a dancer in Harlem, New York, gained fame at the Savoy Ballroom in 1928. Known for its bouncy 6 to 8-count steps, it remained popular throughout the 1930s and 1940s.

ANSWER #28: D) 6

Developed in the 1940s, East Coast Swing evolved from the Lindy Hop and features a basic 6-count pattern with turns and spins. Its popularity soared due to the influence of Arthur Murray's dance studio across the U.S

ANSWER #29: B) Utility Clothing

Utility clothing became popular during World War II as part of the British government's efforts to conserve resources and ensure affordability during the harsh economic climate. The designs were simple and practical, using minimal fabric and materials.

ANSWER #30: C) 1945

Dr. Samwel Charles founded the American Academy of Dental Medicine with the aim of addressing dental and medical issues.

1950s Questions

#1 - WHAT YEAR DID THE SERIES *THE TWILIGHT ZONE* BEGIN AIRING?

A) 1959

C) 1954

B) 1955

D) 1950

#2 - WHICH STATE BECAME THE 49TH STATE IN 1959?

A) Hawaii

C) New Mexico

B) Alaska

D) Texas

#3 - WHICH MINIATURE VEHICLE TOY WAS NAMED IN HONOR OF A LAKE IN MINNESOTA?

A) Tin Toy Robots

B) Lincoln Logs

C) Matchbox Cars

D) Tonka Trucks

#4 - WHICH 1959 NOVEL DETAILS THE HISTORY OF THE HAWAII?

A) From a Native Daughter

C) The Descendants

B) Hawaii

D) The Beginning

#5 - THE NATIONAL LEAGUE OWNERS VOTED ON MAY 28, 1957, TO ALLOW WHICH TWO CLUBS TO MOVE TO NEW CITIES?

A) New York Yankees and New York Giants

C) Brooklyn Dodgers and New York Yankees

B) Philadelphia Phillies and Brooklyn Dodgers

D) New York Giants and Brooklyn Dodgers

#6 - WHICH ACTRESS WON HER FIRST EMMY AWARD NOMINATION FOR HER ROLE IN HER SHOW *LIFE WITH ELIZABETH*?

A) Grace Kelly

C) Betty White

B) Marilyn Monroe

D) Kim Novak

#7 - WHICH BASEBALL PLAYER WAS KNOWN AS "THE SAY HEY KID"?

A) Willie Mays

C) Duke Snider

B) Hank Aaron

D) Alex George

#8 - WHICH 1950S CAR WAS DUBBED THE "HOT ONE"?

A) Porsche 550 Spyder   C) Jaguar XK120

B) Aston Martin DB4 GT Zagato   D) Chevrolet Bel Air

#9 - WHICH BANK BECAME THE FIRST TO ISSUE CREDIT CARDS?

A) Bank of America   C) Wells Fargo

B) Chase Bank   D) Citigroup

#10 - HOW MANY GAME TOKENS WERE INCLUDED IN THE 1950S MONOPOLY VERSION?

A) 8   C) 10

B) 7   D) 11

#11 - WHAT YEAR DID TWO PUERTO RICAN MEN ATTEMPT TO ASSASSINATE PRESIDENT HARRY S. TRUMAN?

A) 1950   C) 1952

B) 1954   D) 1953

#12 - WHAT YEAR WAS THE FIRST MISS AMERICA PAGEANT BROADCAST ON TELEVISION?

A) 1952   C) 1959

B) 1950   D) 1954

#13 - WHO WAS THE DEMOCRATIC CANDIDATE WHO RAN AGAINST EISENHOWER IN THE 1952 AND 1956 PRESIDENTIAL ELECTIONS?

A) Vincent Hallinan

C) John F. Kennedy

B) Adlai E. Stevenson II

D) Lyndon B. Johnson

#14 - WHICH THEME PARK OPENED ON JULY 17, 1955?

A) Story Land

C) Disneyland

B) Mahi Magic

D) Universal Resort

#15 - WHAT SLANG WORD WAS USED IN THE 1950S TO REFER TO EYEGLASSES?

A) Cheaters

C) Turkey

B) Frames

D) Ville

#16 - IN WHICH LANDMARK CASE DID THE U.S. SUPREME COURT RULE THAT RACIAL SEGREGATION OF PUBLIC SCHOOLS WAS UNCONSTITUTIONAL?

A) Loving v. Virginia

C) Plessy v. Ferguson

B) Brown v. Board of Education

D) McCulloch v. Maryland

#17 - WHO SANG THE 1955 ROCK 'N' ROLL HIT "ROCK AROUND THE CLOCK"

A) Bill Haley & His Comets

C) Paul Anka

B) Elvis Presley

D) Little Richard

#18 - WHO WROTE *THE LION, THE WITCH, AND THE WARDROBE*?

A) Ralph Ellison

C) C.S. Lewis

B) Ayn Rand

D) Dr. Seuss

#19 - WHICH ACTOR STARRED IN THE 1951 FILM *BEDTIME FOR BONZO* AND LATER BECAME A FUTURE PRESIDENT?

A) Charles Farrell

C) John F. Kennedy

B) Donald Trump

D) Ronald Reagan

#20 - WHERE WAS THE FIRST HYDROGEN BOMB SUCCESSFULLY DETONATED IN NOVEMBER 1952?

A) Los Alamos

C) New Mexico

B) Marshall Islands

D) Hiroshima

#21 - WHAT POPULAR TOY IN THE 1950S WAS THE FIRST TOY TO BE ADVERTISED ON TV FOR CHILDREN?

A) Barbie

C) Hula Hoop

B) Mr. Potato Head

D) Scooter

#22 - WHAT IS THE NAME OF THE CAKE FROM THE 1950S THAT DID **NOT** INCLUDE EGGS, MILK, OR BUTTER?

A) Chocolate cake

C) Wacky cake

B) Fairy cake

D) Vanilla cake

#23 - WHICH TELEVISION NETWORK AIRED THE WIDELY WATCHED "LUCY GOES TO HOSPITAL" EPISODE FROM THE SERIES *I LOVE LUCY*?

A) CBS

C) ABC

B) NBC

D) FOX

#24 - WHAT IS THE NAME OF A FAMOUS 1950S COCKTAIL KNOWN FOR ITS SWEETNESS AND BABY-PINK HUE?

A) Sea Breeze

C) The Pink Squirrel

B) Sloe Gin Fizz

D) Mai Tai

#25 - WHO WROTE THE BOOK *NOTES OF A NATIVE SON*?

A) Amiri Baraka

C) Maya Angelou

B) W.E.B. Du Bois

D) James Baldwin

#26 - WHAT TERM IS USED IN THE GAME SCRABBLE WHEN A PLAYER SUCCESSFULLY USES ALL SEVEN OF THEIR TILES IN A SINGLE TURN?

A) Fishing

C) Bingo

B) Bonus

D) Phony

#27 - WHAT IS THE NAME OF THE RECORD LABEL OPENED BY SAM PHILLIPS ON MARCH 27, 1952?

A) Decca

C) Capital

B) Columbia

D) Sun Records

#28 - THE DOUBLE HELIX STRUCTURE OF DNA WAS DISCOVERED BY FRANCIS CRICK AND WHICH OTHER SCIENTIST?

A) James Watson

C) Dr. Willem Kolff

B) Charles Laveran

D) Paul Muller

#29 - WHICH BROADCASTING NETWORK AIRED THE FIRST COMMERCIAL COLOR TV PROGRAM?

A) CBS

C) Fox

B) NBC

D) TBS

#30 - WHICH GAME OF THE EARLY 1950S WAS RELEASED IN CONJUNCTION WITH THE DISNEY MOVIE OF THE SAME TITLE?

A) Pinocchio

C) Mickey Mouse

B) Peter Pan

D) Cinderella

#31 - THE ICONIC PLAY *THE CRUCIBLE*, PUBLISHED IN 1953, IS BASED ON WHICH ACTUAL EVENTS?

A) Salem Witch Trials

C) World War II

B) The Holocaust

D) Yellow River flood

#32 - WHAT WAS AMERICAN PLAYER JOHNNY UNITAS KNOWN AS?

A) Golden Boy

C) The Golden Arm

B) The Assassin

D) Beast Mode

#33 - WHICH WORDS WERE ADDED TO THE U.S. PLEDGE OF ALLEGIANCE IN 1954?

A) The Flag of the United States of America

B) Under God

C) To the Flag

D) I Pledge Allegiance

#34 - 1956 SHOW *THE HONEYMOONERS* HAD HOW MANY EPISODES?

A) 100

B) 39

C) 25

D) 59

#35 - WHAT YEAR WAS THE FIRST CHEX MIX RECIPE PRINTED ON THE CHEX CEREAL BOX?

A) 1952

B) 1954

C) 1959

D) 1955

#36 - WHICH 1950S FASHION STYLE FEATURED SLICKED BACK HAIR, BLACK LEATHER JACKETS, AND JEANS?

A) Greasers

B) Beatniks

C) The New Look

D) Ivy League

#37 - WHICH TEAM BECAME THE FIRST IN THE NFL TO ARRANGE FOR ALL OF THEIR GAMES TO BE TELEVISED IN 1950?

A) Los Angeles Rams

C) New York Giants

B) Cleveland Browns

D) Chicago Bears

#38 - WHAT DOES THE SLANG TERM "ANKLE BITER" REFER TO?

A) Shoes

C) Ankle socks

B) Small child

D) Hair

#39 - WHAT YEAR DID THE BARBIE DOLL DEBUT AT THE AMERICAN INTERNATIONAL TOY FAIR IN NEW YORK?

A) 1950

C) 1955

B) 1954

D) 1959

#40 - HOW MANY SEATS DID THE FIRST GENERATION OF THE 1955 FORD THUNDERBIRD CAR HAVE?

A) 2

C) 7

B) 4

D) 6

#41 - HOW MANY ROUNDS ARE THERE IN THE GAME YAHTZEE?

A) 7

C) 10

B) 5

D) 13

#42 - WHAT IS THE NAME OF GWENDOLYN BROOKS' POETRY BOOK THAT WON THE PULITZER PRIZE IN 1950?

A) Annie Allen

C) We Real Cool

B) Maud Martha

D) Blacks

#43 - WHAT STYLE OF EYEGLASSES WAS COMMON IN THE 1950S?

A) Cat Eye

C) Flip-Up

B) Sport

D) Clip-On

#44 - WHO INVENTED THE NBA'S 24-SECOND SHOT CLOCK IN 1954?

A) Murray Mendenhall

C) Danny Biasone

B) Cliff Barker

D) Maurice Podoloff

#45 - WHAT TERM WAS USED IN THE 1950S TO REFER TO A DRIVE-IN MOVIE THEATER?

A) Passion Pits

C) Turkey

B) Daddy-O

D) Apple Butter

#46 - WHAT IS THE TITLE OF THE BOOK THAT INTRODUCED THE CHARACTER, HOLLY GOLIGHTLY?

A) Atlas Shrugged

C) East of Eden

B) Lolita

D) Breakfast at Tiffany's

#47 - ON DECEMBER 28, 1958, BY WHAT SCORE DID THE BALTIMORE COLTS DEFEAT THE NEW YORK GIANTS IN OVERTIME?

A) 23-17

C) 16-13

B) 70-20

D) 13-10

#48 - WHICH ACTOR BECAME THE FIRST-EVER POSTHUMOUS NOMINEE FOR AN ACADEMY AWARD?

A) Heath Ledger

C) Peter Flinch

B) James Dean

D) Howard Ashman

#49 - WHAT DID THE SLANG TERM "DADDY-O" MEAN IN THE 1950S?

A) Cool man

C) Convertible car

B) Dog

D) Leave quickly

#50 - WHAT IS THE NAME OF THE TOY THAT WAS ORIGINALLY CREATED FOR THE 1953 FILM *GUMBASIA*?

A) Mr. Potato Head

C) Mickey Mouse

B) Howdy Doody Monkey

D) Gumby

#51 - WHEN DID NASA ANNOUNCE THE SELECTION OF THE "MERCURY 7"?

A) July 20, 1959

C) June 25, 1958

B) April 9, 1959

D) March 12, 1952

#52 - WHICH TOY COMPANY PRODUCES PLAY-DOH?

A) Hartland Plastics

C) Hasbro

B) American Toy Company

D) Funskool Ltd

#53 - HOW MANY ACADEMY AWARDS DID THE ICONIC 1959 MOVIE *BEN-HUR* RECEIVE?

A) 23

C) 8

B) 11

D) 9

#54 - WHO INVENTED THE POLIO VACCINE IN MARCH 1953?

A) Jonas Salk

C) Almroth Edward Wright

B) Edward Jenner

D) Richard Pfeiffer

#55 - WHAT YEAR DID ACTRESS MARILYN MONROE MARRY RETIRED BASEBALL PLAYER JOE DIMAGGIO?

A) 1952

C) 1954

B) 1953

D) 1955

#56 - WHEN DID THE NOVEL *THE CATCHER IN THE RYE* GET PUBLISHED?

A) July 16, 1951

C) October 15, 1952

B) April 14, 1952

D) October 19, 1953

#57 - IN WHICH YEAR DURING THE 1950S DID THE BOSTON CELTICS WIN THEIR FIRST NBA CHAMPIONSHIP?

A) 1951   C) 1959

B) 1956   D) 1957

#58 - WHICH FAMOUS BOXER RETIRED ON APRIL 27, 1956, BECOMING THE FIRST TO RETIRE UNDEFEATED AS HEAVYWEIGHT CHAMPION?

A) Muhammad Ali   C) Willie Pep

B) Joe Louis   D) Rocky Marciano

#59 - WHAT YEAR DID JACK KILBY AND ROBERT NOYCE INVENT THE MICROCHIP?

A) 1959   C) 1957

B) 1958   D) 1956

#60 - HOW MANY WORLD SERIES DID THE NEW YORK YANKEES APPEAR IN FROM 1949 TO 1960?

A) 3   C) 7

B) 10   D) 5

#61 - WHAT 1954 INVENTION ARE SCIENTISTS GERALD PEARSON, CALVIN FULLER, AND DARYL CHAPIN RECOGNIZED FOR?

A) Solar cell   C) Computer

B) Calculator   D) Fiber optics

#62 - WHO CAME UP WITH THE TOY CORN POPPER?

A) Arthur Holt

C) Harold Graves

B) Erno Rubik

D) Patricia Hogan

#63 - HOW MANY FIRST-GENERATION 1953 CADILLAC ELDORADOS WERE PRODUCED?

A) 200

C) 532

B) 1,575

D) 2,000

#64 - WHAT YEAR DID THE MERCEDES-BENZ 300SL DEBUT?

A) 1957

C) 1959

B) 1954

D) 1950

#65 - WHICH FASHION DESIGNER INTRODUCED THE COLLECTION DUBBED THE "NEW LOOK"?

A) Coco Chanel

C) Christian Dior

B) Pierre Balmain

D) Cristóbal Balenciaga

#66 - IN WHAT YEAR DID THE FAMOUS *THE GEORGE BURNS AND GRACIE ALLEN SHOW* PREMIERE?

A) 1954

C) 1959

B) 1957

D) 1950

#67 - WHAT WAS THE AVERAGE COST OF A WASH AND DRYER UNIT DURING THE 1950S?

A) $300-$400

C) $100- $150

B) $1000-$1200

D) $2000-2500

#68 - WHICH TV BRAND WAS THE MOST WIDELY SOLD IN THE 1950S?

A) Sony

C) Samsung

B) RCA

D) Philips

#69 - WHAT HUMAN ORGAN WAS SUCCESSFULLY TRANSPLANTED FOR THE FIRST TIME IN 1954?

A) Liver

C) Heart

B) Lungs

D) Kidney

#70 - APPROXIMATELY HOW MUCH IN CASH, CHECKS, AND SECURITIES WAS STOLEN DURING THE GREAT BRINK'S ROBBERY?

A) $1 million

C) $1 billion

B) $2 million

D) $750,000

#71 - WHEN DID THE U.S. ENTER THE KOREAN WAR?

A) December 1, 1957

C) July 27, 1953

B) April 25, 1950

D) June 27, 1950

#72 - WHAT TERM IS USED TO DESCRIBE PEOPLE BORN IN THE 1950S?

A) The Greatest Generation

C) The Silent Generation

B) Generation X

D) Baby Boomers

#73 - WHICH AMENDMENT TO THE U.S. CONSTITUTION LIMITS THE NUMBER OF TIMES A PERSON CAN BE ELECTED PRESIDENT?

A) 21st Amendment

C) 23rd Amendment

B) 22nd Amendment

D) 20th Amendment

#74 - WHAT YEAR DID THE U.S. ENTER INTO THE SOUTHEAST ASIA TREATY ORGANIZATION (SEATO) ALLIANCE?

A) 1957

C) 1954

B) 1959

D) 1950

#75 - HOW MANY BLACK STUDENTS ATTENDED CENTRAL HIGH SCHOOL IN LITTLE ROCK AFTER SEGREGATION WAS OUTLAWED?

A) 11

C) 9

B) 2

D) 15

1950s: Answer Key

ANSWER #1: D) 1950

Written by Rod Serling, *The Twilight Zone* was an anthology series that introduced enduring science-fiction themes with actors like George Takei, Cloris Leachman, William Shatner, and Robert Redford. It aired on CBS.

ANSWER #2: B) ALASKA

Alaska, purchased from Russia for $7.2 million, was a U.S. territory before becoming a state. On January 3, 1959, President Eisenhower signed the proclamation admitting Alaska, making it the largest state.

ANSWER #3: D) TONKA TRUCKS

Tonka Toys, originally Mound Metalcraft, rebranded in 1955, with a logo inspired by Lake Minnetonka featuring red over blue waves with seagulls. Tonka Trucks quickly became popular.

ANSWER #4: B) HAWAII

James A. Michener's *Hawaii*, published on November 12, 1959, explores the history and cultural struggles of the Hawaiian people, focusing on their journey to preserve identity and harmony.

ANSWER #5: D) NEW YORK GIANTS AND BROOKLYN DODGERS

Owners unanimously approved moving the New York Giants to San Francisco and the Brooklyn Dodgers to Los Angeles, sparking mixed fan reactions.

ANSWER #6: C) BETTY WHITE

Life with Elizabeth (1952) starred Betty White as Elizabeth. She produced the show, making her the first woman in Hollywood to produce her own sitcom.

ANSWER #7: A) WILLIE MAYS

Willie Mays, nicknamed "The Say Hey Kid," began his career with the New York Giants. A Hall of Famer, he was a two-time MVP and a 24-time All-Star, with a career spanning from the 1950s to the 1970s.

ANSWER #8: D) CHEVROLET BEL AIR

The Chevrolet Bel Air (1950-1975) became iconic for its sleek design and powerful V8 engine. In 1953, it reached 0 to 60 mph in 19.6 seconds.

ANSWER #9: A) BANK OF AMERICA

Bank of America launched the famous BankAmericard in 1966, but the Diners Club card was the first store card to gain widespread use.

ANSWER #10: C) 10

The original set of 10 Monopoly tokens included the battleship, boot, cannon, horse and rider, iron, racecar, dog, thimble, top hat, and wheelbarrow. In 1950, the lantern, rocking horse, and purse were retired.

ANSWER #11: A) 1950

On November 1, 1950, Oscar Collazo and Griselio Torresola attempted an assassination at Blair House. Both were members of the extremist Puerto Rican Nationalist Party, which was fighting for independence.

ANSWER #12: D) 1954

The 1954 Miss America Pageant was aired at 10:30 pm, and 27 million

Americans tuned in to watch the crowning. Miss Evelyn Margaret Ay from Pennsylvania was crowned.

ANSWER #13: B) Adlai E. Stevenson II

Adlai E. Stevenson II received 395,337 votes in 1952 and 372,613 in 1956, both against Dwight D. Eisenhower. Stevenson's grandfather, Adlai E. Stevenson I, was the 23rd Vice President from 1893 to 1897.

ANSWER #14: C) DISNEYLAND

Disneyland opened on July 17, 1955, in Anaheim, California, after one year of construction. Featuring five themed lands and 20 attractions, it was the only theme park designed and built under Walt Disney's direct supervision.

ANSWER #15: A) CHEATERS

The term "cheaters" lightheartedly implies that the glasses provide a way to cheat by improving vision. Although it originated in the 1920s, it was also a common term in the 1950s. To some, the term was also slang for sunglasses.

ANSWER #16: B) BROWN V. BOARD OF EDUCATION

On May 17, 1954, the U.S. Supreme Court, led by Justice Earl Warren, unanimously ruled in Brown v. Board of Education that segregation in public schools violated the 14th Amendment. This overturned the 1896 Plessy v. Ferguson case, which had upheld the "separate but equal" doctrine.

ANSWER #17: A) BILL HALEY & HIS COMETS

"Rock Around the Clock" became the first rock song to hit the Billboard Pop chart, where it stayed for eight weeks. It is estimated that 25 million copies were sold.

ANSWER #18: C) C.S. LEWIS

The Lion, the Witch, and the Wardrobe was first published in 1950 and is the first and most famous book of C.S. Lewis's Chronicles of Narnia series.

ANSWER #19: D) RONALD REAGAN

Before becoming president in 1981, Ronald Reagan was a well-known actor in Hollywood, and his acting career spanned over 30 years. Reagan starred as Professor Peter Boyd, where he tries to teach ethics to a chimpanzee.

ANSWER #20: B) MARSHALL ISLANDS

The first thermonuclear weapon, code-named Mike, was tested on November 1, 1952, at Eniwetok Atoll in the Marshall Islands, briefly giving the U.S. an edge in the nuclear arms race until the Soviet Union's test the next year.

ANSWER #21: B) MR. POTATO HEAD

Invented in 1949 by George Lerner and later manufactured in 1952 by Hasbro, Mr. Potato Head was a toy that children could design themselves.

ANSWER #22: C) WACKY CAKE

Wacky Cake, or vinegar cake, became popular after the Great Depression due to scarce ingredients, and it remained a 1950s favorite.

ANSWER #23: A) CBS

On January 19, 1953, "Lucy Goes to Hospital" aired on CBS, with 68% of U.S. households tuning in to watch the birth of Little Ricky. That same night, Lucille Ball gave birth to her second child.

ANSWER #24: C) THE PINK SQUIRREL

Created in 1941 at Bryant's Cocktail Lounge in Milwaukee, the Pink Squirrel gained 1950s fame through TV sitcoms. It's made with crème de noyau, white crème de cacao, and heavy cream..

ANSWER #25: D) JAMES BALDWIN

Notes of a Native Son, written in the 1940s and 1950s, offers insight into the U.S. social climate during the Civil Rights Movement. Baldwin later wrote other influential essays like "Nobody Knows My Name."

ANSWER #26: C) BINGO

Scrabble, created by Alfred Mosher Butts and refined by James Brunot, is a word game where players build words with seven letter tiles. Its 1950s popularity led to licensing with Selchow and Righter for broader distribution.

ANSWER #27: D) SUN RECORDS

Sun Records, opened on March 27, 1952, in Memphis, used the slogan: "We Record Anything—Anywhere—Anytime." The label later discovered Elvis Presley, releasing five of his singles.

ANSWER #28: A) JAMES WATSON

DNA was first identified in the 1860s by Friedrich Miescher, with later scientists uncovering more about its structure. James Watson and Francis Crick discovered the DNA molecule's three-dimensional double helix shape.

ANSWER #29: A) CBS

On June 25, 1951, CBS aired the first color TV program, though few could watch it due to most people owning black-and-white sets. CBS then began the first regular color TV series, *The World Is Yours!*, on June 27, 1951.

ANSWER #30: B) PETER PAN

Released in 1953, the game lets players choose between Peter Pan, Michael, Wendy, or John Darling. The goal is to be the first to travel from the Darling's House to Neverland and back.

ANSWER #31: A) SALEM WITCH TRIALS

The Crucible is a four-act play that dramatizes the 1692 Salem witch trials, although it is partially fictionalized. It was published in 1953 during the height of the Second Red Scare.

ANSWER #32: C) THE GOLDEN ARM

Born in 1933, in Pittsburgh, John Unitas, known as "The Golden Arm," is regarded as one of the greatest quarterbacks of the 20th century. He led the Baltimore Colts to three NFL championships and a Super Bowl win in 1971.

ANSWER #33: B) UNDER GOD

In June 1954, President Eisenhower signed a bill adding "Under God" to the Pledge of Allegiance to distinguish the U.S. ideologically from the Soviet Union. Two years later, he made "In God We Trust" the official U.S. motto.

ANSWER #34: B) 39

The Honeymooners, created by Jackie Gleason, ran for 39 episodes and followed two working-class Brooklyn couples. Art Carney and Audrey Meadows won Emmys for their roles.

ANSWER #35: A) 1952

Chex Mix gained popularity at parties for its crunchy, salty blend. The original recipe mixed Chex cereal with nuts, Worcestershire sauce, butter, garlic salt, and salt, then baked before cooling.

ANSWER #36: A) GREASERS

Greasers wore dark jeans, T-shirts, leather jackets, and boots, with greased-back hair styled using pomade or petroleum jelly. This style became iconic with rock 'n' roll stars like Elvis Presley.

ANSWER #37: A) LOS ANGELES RAMS

The Rams were the first NFL team to televise their games, with DuMont network paying $75,000 for the rights.

ANSWER #38: C) SMALL CHILD

The slang term "ankle-biter" originally referred to small children, who are small enough to reach a person's ankles. The term later also came to describe small animals like dogs.

ANSWER #39: D) 1959

Barbie debuted on March 9, 1959, created by Ruth Handler, inspired by the German Lilli doll. Within its first year, Barbie sold 300,000 units.

ANSWER #40: A) 2

The 1955 Ford Thunderbird, a personal luxury car, debuted on October 22, 1954, and quickly became a hit, endorsed by celebrities like Marilyn Monroe.

ANSWER #41: D) 13

Yahtzee has 13 rounds, where players roll dice and record results in 13 categories, each used only once. The game was introduced in the 1950s.

ANSWER #42: A) ANNIE ALLEN

Annie Allen is a poetry series about an African American girl in Chicago.

Gwendolyn Brooks won the Pulitzer Prize for it in 1950, the first Black person to do so.

ANSWER #43: A) CAT EYE

The Cat Eye style features rounded frames with an upswept design, resembling a cat's eyes. It was popularized by stars like Audrey Hepburn.

ANSWER #44: C) DANNY BIASONE

Danny Biasone, owner of the Syracuse Nationals, introduced the 24-second shot clock to speed up NBA games. This rule led to faster play and higher scores, boosting fan interest.

ANSWER #45: A) PASSION PITS

Drive-in theaters, popular in the 1950s, offered a mix of communal movie-watching and car privacy, making them ideal date spots. This led to the slang term "Passion Pits.

ANSWER #46: D) BREAKFAST AT TIFFANY'S

Holly Golightly, from Truman Capote's 1958 novella *Breakfast at Tiffany's*, is an independent young woman who dates wealthy men for support. The story follows her search for freedom amid personal crises.

ANSWER #47: A) 23-17

On December 28, 1958, the Baltimore Colts defeated the New York Giants 23-17 in the NFL Championship, in what's often called the greatest game ever played. It was the first NFL game to go into overtime, with 45 million viewers tuning in.

ANSWER #48: B) JAMES DEAN

James Dean died on September 30, 1955, at age 24 in a car accident. He starred in three major films before his death and received posthumous Best Actor nominations in 1956 and 1957 for *East of Eden* and *Giant*.

ANSWER #49: A) COOL MAN

Popular in the 1950s, this term was used to call someone cool. Jazz singers often used it on stage too.

ANSWER #50: D) GUMBY

Gumby, created by Art Clokey, debuted in the short film *Gumbasia* and became so popular that it led to *The Gumby Show* and a beloved toy in 1955.

ANSWER #51: B) APRIL 9, 1959

The "Mercury Seven" astronauts were introduced on April 9, 1959, and included Scott Carpenter, John Glenn, and Alan Shepard.

ANSWER #52: C) HASBRO

Play-Doh, originally a wallpaper cleaner, was repurposed for modeling and later became a popular toy. It was sold to Hasbro and debuted as a modeling compound in 1956.

ANSWER #53: B) 11

Ben-Hur, a film about a Jewish prince enslaved by the Romans, won 11 of its 12 Academy Award nominations. Known for its iconic chariot race, it was the most expensive film of its time, costing $15 million to make.

ANSWER #54: A) JONAS SALK

Jonas Salk developed the polio vaccine in 1953, testing it on himself, his family, and later 1.6 million children. He chose not to patent the vaccine, making it widely accessible.

ANSWER #55: C) 1954

Marilyn Monroe and Joe DiMaggio, a legendary power couple, married on January 14, 1954, at San Francisco City Hall. Despite their iconic status, the marriage lasted just nine months.

ANSWER #56: A) July 16, 1951

Written by J.D. Salinger and published by Little, Brown and Company, *The Catcher in the Rye* challenges readers to expand their comfort zones while upholding personal values. The book has sold over 65 million copies.

ANSWER #57: D) 1957

The Boston Celtics won their first NBA Championship in 1957, defeating the St. Louis Hawks in a thrilling seven-game series. This victory marked the beginning of the Celtics' dominance in the NBA during the late 1950s and 1960s.

ANSWER #58: D) ROCKY MARCIANO

Rocky Marciano, famed for his power, went undefeated in 49 fights after starting his career in 1947. He retired at 32 after six successful title defenses.

ANSWER #59: A) 1959

Jack Kilby, at Texas Instruments, created the first integrated circuit with Robert Noyce, who later co-founded Intel, a leading microchip manufacturer.

ANSWER #60: B) 10

The New York Yankees appeared in 10 World Series between 1949 and 1960, winning seven. Under manager Casey Stengel, they secured five consecutive titles from 1949 to 1953.

ANSWER #61: A) SOLAR CELL

On April 25, 1954, Bell Labs announced the invention of the solar cell and demonstrated it by using their solar panel to power a small toy Ferris wheel.

ANSWER #62: A) ARTHUR HOLT

Arthur Holt designed the Corn Popper, a toy that creates a popping sound as it propels colorful balls. Holt sold the design to Fisher-Price for $50.

ANSWER #63: C) 532

Only 532 first-generation Eldorados were made, making them rare collectibles today. Priced at $8,000 in 1953, they came in four colors: Azure Blue, Aztec Red, Alpine White, and Artisan Ochre.

ANSWER #64: B) 1954

The Mercedes-Benz 300 SL debuted in February 1954 at the International Motor Sport Show in New York. Its racing success and innovative design quickly made it an icon.

ANSWER #65: C) CHRISTIAN DIOR

In February 1947, Christian Dior introduced the "New Look," emphasizing a tiny waist and full hips. This elegant style quickly gained popularity post-war due to consumers' increased spending power.

ANSWER #66: D) 1950

The *George Burns and Gracie Allen Show*, starring the real-life couple, aired from 1950 to 1958, earning multiple Emmy nominations.

ANSWER #67: A) $300-$400

The electric washer and dryer, which simplified laundry, became popular in the 1950s as post-war purchasing power increased.

ANSWER #68: B) RCA

The 1950s, the golden age of TV, saw RCA as a leading brand in American homes. Their televisions, ranging from 15 to 21 inches, were priced between $200 and $600.

ANSWER #69: D) KIDNEY

In 1954, Boston's Peter Bent Brigham Hospital performed the first successful kidney transplant between identical twins. This breakthrough paved the way for future organ transplants.

ANSWER #70: B) $2 MILLION

On January 17, 1950, the Great Brink's Robbery took place in Boston, where robbers stole $2 million in cash. Known as the "crime of the century," only $58,000 was recovered, despite all 11 robbers being identified by 1956.

ANSWER #71: D) JUNE 27, 1950

The Korean War began on June 25, 1950, with North Korea's invasion of South Korea. Two days later, on June 27, 1950, the United States entered the conflict as a UN member, supporting South Korea against the communist-backed North.

ANSWER #72: D) BABY BOOMERS

Baby Boomers are defined by the post-World War II surge in births, with about 76 million babies born between 1946 and 1964. This population boom was largely due to the improved living conditions and optimism following the war.

ANSWER #73: B) 22ND AMENDMENT

Ratified on February 27, 1951, the 22nd Amendment limits U.S. presidents to two terms. This formalized the precedent set by George Washington, although no specific event triggered its creation.

ANSWER #74: C) 1954

Formed in September 1954, SEATO included the U.S., New Zealand, Australia, and others to counter communism in Southeast Asia. The alliance dissolved in 1977 after members began withdrawing in the 1970s.

ANSWER #75: C) 9

On September 4, 1957, the Little Rock Nine faced a hostile mob while attempting to attend Central High School. President Eisenhower sent federal troops to ensure their safe passage, highlighting the fight for desegregation and civil rights.

1960s Questions

#1 - IN WHICH U.S. STATE WAS PRESIDENT JOHN F. KENNEDY ASSASSINATED?

A) Texas

C) Arizona

B) California

D) Florida

#2 - WHO RELEASED THE SINGLE "WHAT A WONDERFUL WORLD" IN 1967?

A) Ella Fitzgerald

C) Billie Holiday

B) Louis Armstrong

D) Duke Ellington

#3 - WHICH AMERICAN CIVIL RIGHTS LEADER DELIVERED THE FAMOUS "I HAVE A DREAM" SPEECH IN 1963?

A) Roy Wilkins

C) James Farmer

B) Martin Luther King Junior

D) John Lewis

#4 - WHAT DOES THE WORD "FUZZ" MEAN?

A) Doctors

C) Nurses

B) Teachers

D) Police

#5 - WHO PLAYED "BATMAN" IN THE 1966 TELEVISION SERIES?

A) Tommy Cruiz

C) Adam West

B) Sean Connery

D) Paul Newman

#6 - WHICH FASHION TREND WAS LINKED TO SINGER NANCY SINATRA?

A) Mood rings

C) Culottes

B) Go-go boots

D) Tie-dye shirts

#7 - WHICH OF THESE ACTRESSES PLAYED A ROLE IN THE EPIC 1963 FILM *CLEOPATRA*?

A) Julie Andrews

C) Doris Day

B) Jane Fonda

D) Elizabeth Taylor

#8 - WHICH OF THESE WAS **NOT** A GADGET OF THE '60S?

A) Television

C) Cassette Tape

B) Radio

D) Computer

#9 - WHICH 1960S ATHLETE WAS KNOWN AS 'THE GREATEST?'

A) Wilt Chamberlain

C) Muhammad Ali

B) Roy Emerson

D) Bobby Hull

#10 – IN WHICH YEAR DID THE ICONIC ACTRESS AND MODEL MARILYN MONROE DIE?

A) 1968

C) 1962

B) 1960

D) 1961

#11 - WHICH YEAR WAS THE HIT "CALIFORNIA DREAMIN" RELEASED?

A) 1961

C) 1969

B) 1968

D) 1965

#12 - WHO WAS PRESIDENT JOHN F. KENNEDY'S VICE PRESIDENT?

A) Lyndon B. Johnson

C) Spiro Agnew

B) Gerald Ford

D) Richard Nixon

#13 - WHICH OF THESE 1960S SLANG WAS USED TO DESCRIBE A HOUSE OR AN APARTMENT?

A) Pad

C) Crib

B) Abode

D) Spot

#14 - WHICH YEAR DID THE WORLD SERIES END BY A HOME RUN FOR THE FIRST TIME?

A) 1955

C) 1960

B) 1961

D) 1970

#15 - WHICH OF THESE WAS FORMERLY KNOWN AS CRISPHEAD LETTUCE?

A) Iceberg Lettuce

C) Plain Lettuce

B) Beef Wellington

D) Swedish Lettuce

#16 - WHICH YEAR WAS MEDICARE HEALTH INSURANCE INTRODUCED FOR AMERICANS OVER 65 YEARS?

A) 1965

C) 1960

B) 1966

D) 1968

#17 - WHICH OF THESE FASHION TRENDS WAS POPULARIZED BY JACKIE KENNEDY IN THE '60S?

A) Mini Skirt

C) Bell-bottom jeans

B) Pillbox hat

D) Capri trousers

#18 - WHAT IS THE MAXIMUM NUMBER OF PLAYERS THAT CAN PLAY THE GREEN GHOST BOARD GAME?

A) 12

C) 13

B) 8

D) 4

#19 - WHICH OF THESE TREATMENTS WAS **NOT** INTRODUCED IN THE 1960S TO FIGHT LEUKEMIA?

A) Blood transfusion

C) Steroids

B) Chemotherapy

D) Radiation

#20 - WHAT WAS THE NAME OF THE FIRST JAMES BOND MOVIE RELEASED IN THE 1960S?

A) Goldfinger

C) Thunderball

B) Dr. No

D) From Russia with Love

#21 - WHICH AMERICAN CAR WON THE FAMOUS LE MANS ENDURANCE RACE FOUR YEARS IN A ROW?

A) Ford GT40

C) Shelby Cobra

B) Ford Galaxie

D) Aston Martin DB5

#22 - UNDER WHOSE ADMINISTRATION DID THE CUBAN MISSILE CRISIS TAKE PLACE?

A) Ronald Reagan

C) John F. Kennedy

B) Jimmy Carter

D) Richard Nixon

#23 - WHICH OF THE FOLLOWING POLITICAL FIGURES WAS **NOT** ASSASSINATED?

A) John F. Kennedy

B) Bobby Kennedy

C) Martin Luther King Jr

D) Richard Nixon

#24 - WHICH SINGER POPULARIZED THE TWIST DANCE IN 1960?

A) Chubby Checker

B) Teri Garr

C) Joey Dee

D) Steve McQueen

#25 – "HACKER" WAS USED TO DESCRIBE A PERSON ATTEMPTING TO ACCESS A NETWORK FOR WHICH DEVICE?

A) Telephone

B) Computers

C) PlayStation

D) Radio

#26 - THE 1969 NOVEL *THE GODFATHER* WAS WRITTEN BY WHO?

A) Mario Puzo

B) Penelope Fitzgerald

C) Douglas Adams

D) Jonathan Swift

#27 - WHICH '60S TOY HAD A BOUNCING SENSATION?

A) Frisbee

B) Duncan Yo-Yo

C) Wham-O Super Ball

D) Lego Blocks

#28 - WHICH RADIO PERSONALITY IS REFERRED TO AS THE "THE HULLABALOOER"?

A) Dick Biondi

C) Don Steele

B) Bruce Morrow

D) Dave Hull

#29 - WHICH U.S. POLITICAL FIGURE SERVED AS BOTH PRESIDENT AND VICE PRESIDENT IN THE '60S?

A) Jimmy Carter

C) Lyndon B. Johnson

B) Richard Nixon

D) Ronald Reagan

#30 - WHICH OF THE FOLLOWING STARRED IN THE FAMOUS MOVIE *VIVA LAS VEGAS*?

A) Elvis Presley

C) Marilyn Monroe

B) Michael Jackson

D) Buddy Holly

#31 - WHICH OF THE FOLLOWING PRESENTERS WAS NOT A MEMBER OF THE *CROSBY-CLOONEY SHOW*?

A) Bing Crosby

C) Casey Kasem

B) Rosemary Clooney

D) Buddy Cole

#32 - WHAT 1962 DANCE INVOLVED DANCING IN A CHAIN FORMATION ON THE FLOOR LIKE A TRAIN?

A) The Locomotion

C) The Hully Gully

B) The Twist

D) The Wah-Watusi

#33 - WHICH BASEBALL TEAM WAS FOUNDED IN 1962?

A) New York Mets

C) Atlanta Braves

B) Los Angeles Dodgers

D) Houston Astros

#34 - WHAT DID THE TERM "DIG IT" MEAN IN THE 1960S?

A) Disagreeing

C) Disputing

B) Annoying

D) Understanding

#35 - WHICH OF THESE IS A CULINARY TREND OF THE 1960S?

A) Tunnel of fudge cake

C) The cupcake craze

B) Foam and gels

D) Sushi

#36 - WHICH ELECTRONIC GADGET WAS FIRST INTRODUCED IN THE 1960S?

A) Countertop microwave ovens

C) Electric coffee percolators

B) Crockpots

D) Popcorn poppers

#37 - WHICH SWIMMER SET THE FIRST AMERICAN RECORD IN THE 100-YARD BUTTERFLY IN 1967?

A) Lance Larson

C) Esther Williams

B) Mark Spitz

D) Max Ritter

#38 - WHICH SPRINTER WAS THE FIRST AMERICAN WOMAN TO WIN THREE GOLD MEDALS IN ONE OLYMPICS?

A) Debi Thomas

C) Wilma Rudolph

B) Sheryl Swoopes

D) Tidye Pickett

#39 - WHICH HUMAN ORGAN WAS FIRST TRANSPLANTED IN 1963?

A) Heart

C) Liver

B) Kidney

D) Blood

#40 - WHICH DRINK WAS TAKEN TO SPACE BY GEMINI ASTRONAUTS IN 1962?

A) Manhattan

C) Tang

B) Mint Julep

D) Sidecar

#41 - WHO WROTE THE BOOK *A WRINKLE IN TIME*?

A) Joseph Heller

C) Maurice Sendak

B) Madeleine L 'Engle

D) Harper Lee

#42 - WHICH COCKTAIL WAS KNOWN AS "THE OFFICIAL DRINK OF NEW ORLEANS?"

A) Sazerac Cocktail

C) Dirty Martini

B) Sidecar

D) Mai Tai

#43 - IN WHICH YEAR DID GENERAL ELECTRIC INTRODUCE THE FIRST SELF-CLEANING OVEN?

A) 1960

C) 1963

B) 1968

D) 1965

#44 - WHICH 1960S HOLLYWOOD STAR WAS KNOWN AS "THE KING OF COOL"?

A) Burt Lancaster

C) Laurence Olivier

B) Steve McQueen

D) Marcello Mastroianni

#45 - IN WHAT YEAR DID CHEVROLET INTRODUCE THE CORVETTE STINGRAY?

A) 1960

C) 1968

B) 1965

D) 1963

#46 - WHICH YEAR WAS THE ORAL POLIO VACCINE FIRST INTRODUCED IN THE UNITED STATES?

A) 1965

C) 1968

B) 1960

D) 1964

#47 - IN WHICH 1960S TELEVISION SHOW DID ELIZABETH MONTGOMERY PLAY THE ROLE OF A WITCH?

A) Bewitched

C) Bonanza

B) Star Trek

D) The Addams Family

#48 - WHO WAS THE FIRST AMERICAN TO ORBIT THE EARTH IN 1962?

A) Buzz Aldrin

C) Neil Armstrong

B) John Glenn

D) Alan Shepard

#49 - WHICH 1960S RADIO PERSONALITY WAS KNOWN AS THE "FIFTH BEATLE?"

A) Don Steele

C) Dr. Don Rose

B) Murray the K

D) Robert Morgan

#50 - WHICH YEAR DID AT&T PROPOSE 911 AS A NATIONAL EMERGENCY SERVICE NUMBER?

A) 1966

C) 1969

B) 1968

D) 1960

#51 - WHICH OF THESE CARTOON SHORTS WAS **NOT** PART OF *THE PINK PANTHER SHOW*?

A) The Pink Panther

C) A cartoon cat

B) Mister Magoo

D) The Inspector

#52 - WHO DESIGNED THE FAMOUS TOPLESS BATHING SUIT?

A) Rudi Gernreich

C) Mary Quant

B) Andre Courreges

D) Anne Klein

#53 - WHICH HOLLYWOOD STAR WAS THE FIRST BLACK ACTOR TO WIN AN OSCAR FOR BEST ACTOR?

A) Harry Belafonte

C) James Earl Jones

B) Richard Pryor

D) Sidney Poitier

#54 - WHAT COMPANY MADE THE FAMOUS 1962 VINTAGE CANDY LAND BOARD GAME?

A) Milton Bradley

C) Wham-O

B) Mattel

D) Fisher-Price

#55 - WHAT IS THE NAME OF HAYLEY MILLS' FIRST DISNEY MOVIE?

A) The Apartment

C) Pollyanna

B) Snow White

D) Sink the Bismarck

#56 - WHAT 1960S DANCE WAS REFERRED TO AS "THE HALLOWEEN CLASSIC FAVORITE"

A) The Swim

C) The Monster Mash

B) The Hully Gully

D) The Locomotion

#57 - IN WHICH YEAR WAS THE FIRST SUPER BOWL HELD?

A) 1955

C) 1970

B) 1967

D) 1981

#58 - WHO WAS THE NARRATOR IN THE OSCAR-WINNING FILM, *THE BIBLE: IN THE BEGINNING...*

A) John Huston

C) John Wayne

B) Lee Marvin

D) Peter O'Toole

#59 - THE FAMOUS 1960S SLANG "BIPPY" USED TO MEAN "REAR END" ORIGINATED FROM WHICH TV SHOW?

A) The Munsters

C) Rowan and Martin's Laugh-In

B) Duet

D) Scorpion

#60 - WHO WAS THE REPUBLICAN NOMINEE FOR PRESIDENT IN THE 1965 ELECTION?

A) Lyndon Johnson

C) Richard Nixon

B) Barry Goldwater

D) Hubert Humphrey

#61 - WHO CREATED "THE PONY" DANCE?

A) Dee Dee

C) Major Lance

B) Bobby Picket

D) Chubby Checker

#62 - WHEN WAS THE AUTOBIOGRAPHY OF MALCOLM X PUBLISHED?

A) 1968

C) 1961

B) 1966

D) 1965

#63 - WHICH 1960S RADIO PERSONALITY WAS NICKNAMED THE "WILD ITALIAN?"

A) Dick Biondi

C) Don Steele

B) Wolfman Jack

D) Casey Kasem

#64 - IN WHICH VEHICLE WAS PRESIDENT KENNEDY ASSASSINATED?

A) Cadillac Escalade

C) Lincoln Continental

B) Chevy Tahoe

D) Ford F150

#65 - WHICH 1960S SHOW WAS OVERTHROWN BY *THE SIMPSONS* AS THE LONGEST-RUNNING PRIME-TIME CARTOON?

A) The Virginian

C) My Partner the Ghost

B) Benny Hill

D) The Flintstones

#66 - IN WHICH YEAR WAS THE FIRST AND ONLY FASHION SHOW HELD IN THE WHITE HOUSE?

A) 1970

C) 1966

B) 1968

D) 1961

#67 - WHICH NASCAR DRIVER WON HIS SECOND CONSECUTIVE SEASON CHAMPIONSHIP IN 1963?

A) Bill Massay

C) Tommy Herbert

B) Dave Marcus

D) Joe Weatherly

#68 - WHICH OF THESE '60S DANCES WAS INVENTED FOR THE BATMAN TELEVISION SERIES?

A) Twist

C) Batusi

B) Pony

D) Swim

#69 - WHICH ORGANIZATION IN THE UNITED STATES INVENTED THE WEATHER SATELLITE IN 1960?

A) Space X

C) Department of Defense

B) U.S Space Force

D) NASA

#70 - THE FIRST ATM IN THE UNITED STATES WAS INSTALLED IN WHICH STATE?

A) Texas

C) California

B) Utah

D) New York

#71 - WHO AMONG THE FOLLOWING DID **NOT** STAR IN THE 1960 FILM *THE APARTMENT*?

A) Ray Walston

C) Shirley MacLaine

B) Jack Lemmon

D) Kirk Douglas

#72 - WHICH OF WILLIAM FAULKNER'S NOVELS WAS PUBLISHED IN 1962 POSTHUMOUSLY?

A) Sanctuary

C) As I Lay Dying

B) The Reivers

D) Intruder in the Dust

#73 - *THE ADVENTURERS* FILM WAS AN ADAPTATION OF A NOVEL BY WHICH AUTHOR?

A) Sean Desmond

C) Harold Robbins

B) Wally Ferris

D) Nick Hornby

#74 - WHICH YEAR WAS THE HEADACHE BOARD GAME INTRODUCED?

A) 1960

C) 1966

B) 1961

D) 1968

#75 - WHAT WAS THE FIRST ANIMATED TELEVISION SPECIAL PRODUCED BY CHARLES M. SCHULZ AND BILL MELENDEZ, WHICH AIRED IN 1965?

A) Rudolph the Red-Nosed Reindeer

C) A Charlie Brown Christmas

D) Frosty the Snowman

B) How the Grinch Stole Christmas

1960s: Answer Key

ANSWER #1: A) TEXAS

On November 22, 1963, President John F. Kennedy was assassinated while riding through Dealey Plaza in Dallas. Lee Harvey Oswald, accused of the crime, was killed two days later.

ANSWER #2: B) LOUIS ARMSTRONG

"What a Wonderful World" was recorded by Louis Armstrong in 1967, written by Bob Thiele and George David Weiss. The song gained widespread fame after being featured in the 1987 film *Good Morning, Vietnam.*

ANSWER #3: B) MARTIN LUTHER KING JUNIOR

Martin Luther King Junior is globally known for leading the civil rights movement in the U.S. His famous "I Have a Dream" speech was delivered on August 28, 1963, during the march on Washington.

ANSWER #4: D) POLICE

"Fuzz" was a 1960s slang term for the police, often used by hippies. The term, originally used for a "lack of hair," likely originated from a mispronunciation of "the police force."

ANSWER #5: C) ADAM WEST

The 1966–1968 Batman TV series, starring Adam West as Batman, premiered on January 12, 1966, on ABC. This role boosted West's career, leading to key roles in films like *Family Guy* and *Chicken Little.*

ANSWER #6: B) GO-GO BOOTS

Nancy Sinatra's 1966 hit "These Boots Are Made for Walkin'" topped U.S. and UK charts. Her performances in go-go boots popularized the trend.

ANSWER #7: D) ELIZABETH TAYLOR

Elizabeth Taylor, Hollywood's highest-paid star in the 1960s, gained fame for her role as Cleopatra in the 1963 film.

ANSWER #8: D) COMPUTER

In the 1960s, consumer gadgets like cassette recorders, color TVs, radios, and calculators became popular. Telephones also evolved from rotary to push-button designs.

ANSWER #9: C) MUHAMMAD ALI

Muhammad Ali, born Cassius Clay, was a legendary boxer and social activist. He was the first to win the world heavyweight championship three times, defending his title 19 times.

ANSWER #10: C) 1962

Marilyn Monroe, the iconic actress known for her comedic roles, was found dead at her Los Angeles home on August 5, 1962. The cause was determined to be an overdose.

ANSWER #11: D) 1965

"California Dreamin'," a 1960s hit by The Mamas and the Papas, was written by John and Michelle Phillips. Released in December 1965, the song reflects their experiences living in New York City.

ANSWER #12: A) LYNDON B. JOHNSON

After President Kennedy was assassinated on November 22, 1963, Vice President Lyndon B. Johnson was sworn in as the 36th President.

ANSWER #13: A) PAD

The 1960s were famous for having certain expressions that were used to describe everyday things and activities. "Pad" was a famous slang in the '60s that was used to describe a house, an apartment, or any place of residence.

ANSWER #14: C) 1960

The 1960 World Series was held on October 13, 1960. The match was between The Pittsburgh Pirates and the New York Yankees. Bill Mazeroski's walk-off home run won the championship for the Pittsburgh Pirates.

ANSWER #15: A) ICEBERG LETTUCE

Iceberg lettuce, with its pale green, cabbage-like head, became widely popular in the U.S. due to its crispy texture and neutral taste. By the 1950s and 1960s, it was the most commonly grown lettuce in the country.

ANSWER #16: A) 1965

Medicare, a federal health insurance program, was established on June 30, 1965, by legislation signed by President Lyndon B. Johnson. It primarily covers Americans aged 65 and older, as well as younger individuals with certain disabilities.

ANSWER #17: B) PILLBOX HAT

The pillbox hat, a small, brimless, round hat with a flat crown, gained popularity in the 1930s. However, it became iconic in the 1960s when First Lady Jackie Kennedy made it a fashion trend.

ANSWER #18: D) 4

Released in 1965 by Transogram, the Green Ghost board game was the first designed to be played in the dark. It accommodates up to four players and features three boxes with lockable trap doors beneath a glowing plastic board.

ANSWER #19: A) BLOOD TRANSFUSION

Leukemia, known as blood cancer, starts in white blood cells. In the 1960s, treatments advanced with the official use of multi-agent chemotherapy, along with the introduction of steroids and radiation therapy.

ANSWER #20: B) Dr. No

"Dr. No," released in 1962, was the debut James Bond film starring Sean Connery. It introduced the iconic spy, along with the famous theme song, gadgets, and the legendary line, "Bond, James Bond."

ANSWER #21: A) FORD GT40

The Ford GT40, a high-performance race car, was designed for European sports races, with only 105 units produced. It became the first American car to win the Le Mans endurance race, achieving victory four consecutive times from 1966 to 1969.

ANSWER #22: C) JOHN F. KENNEDY

In October 1962, President John F. Kennedy led the U.S. during the Cuban Missile Crisis, a tense 13-day standoff with the Soviet Union over nuclear missiles in Cuba. This confrontation marked one of the Cold War's most critical moments.

ANSWER #23: D) RICHARD NIXON

The 1960s were marked by the tragic assassinations of key leaders: President John F. Kennedy (1963), Malcolm X (1965), Martin Luther King Jr. (1968), and Robert F. Kennedy (1968). These events deeply impacted the political and civil rights landscape in the U.S.

ANSWER #24: A) CHUBBY CHECKER

Chubby Checker, an American singer and dancer, skyrocketed to fame with his 1960 hit "The Twist," which popularized the Twist dance. His follow-up, "Let's Twist Again," cemented the dance craze nationwide.

ANSWER #25: A) TELEPHONE

Originally, "hacker" referred to a tool or a bad golfer, but in the 1960s, it began to describe someone trying to access telephone networks without authorization.

ANSWER #26: A) MARIO PUZO

Published in 1969, *The Godfather* by Mario Puzo is one of the most successful novels ever. It introduced the iconic phrase "I'll make him an offer he can't refuse" and was adapted into a 1972 film by Puzo and Francis Ford Coppola.

ANSWER #27: C) WHAM-O SUPER BALL

Created in the 1960s, the Wham-O Superball was made from a material called Zectron, allowing it to bounce extremely high. The NFL reportedly named the "Super Bowl" after this popular toy.

ANSWER #28: D) DAVE HULL

Dave Hull, known as "The Hullabaloo," was a legendary radio DJ who gained fame at WONE in Ohio. His popularity led to a fan-written song and a custom Baskin-Robbins ice cream flavor in his honor.

ANSWER #29: B) RICHARD NIXON

Richard Nixon became the 37th U.S. President in 1969, previously serving as Vice President under Eisenhower. He resigned from office in 1974 due to the Watergate scandal, making him the first U.S. President to do so.

ANSWER #30: A) ELVIS PRESLEY

Viva Las Vegas is a famous 1964 film about two race car drivers competing for the same girl. Directed by George Sidney and written by Sally Benson, the film stars the legendary singer Elvis Presley as Lucky Jackson.

ANSWER #31: C) CASEY KASEM

The Bing Crosby-Rosemary Clooney Show, airing from 1960 to 1962, was a 20-minute talk radio program aimed at female listeners. It featured Bing Crosby, Rosemary Clooney, and Buddy Cole.

ANSWER #32: A) THE LOCOMOTION

"The Locomotion" dance was inspired by Little Eva's 1962 hit song "The Loco-Motion." The dance mimicked a train, with dancers forming a chain and moving in unison.

ANSWER #33: A) NEW YORK METS

New York Mets are a professional baseball team based in New York. Founded in 1962, the team won two World Series championships in 1969 and 1986. They also won five National League pennants. The team colors are blue and orange.

ANSWER #34: D) UNDERSTANDING

By the 1960s, "understanding" had two meanings: to "understand" something and as an expression of enthusiasm or agreement, signaling that one was on board with an idea or plan.

ANSWER #35: A) TUNNEL OF FUDGE CAKE

Tunnel of Fudge Cake is a chocolate cake with a fudgy center and walnut pieces, topped with a chocolate glaze. It became popular in the 1960s after being featured in Pillsbury's 17th Annual Bake-Off.

ANSWER #36: A) COUNTERTOP MICROWAVE OVENS

Introduced in the 1960s, countertop microwave ovens revolutionized cooking by offering a quick and efficient way to heat food using microwave radiation. Their convenience made them a household staple.

ANSWER #37: B) MARK SPITZ

Mark Spitz, an American swimmer, was the first to win seven gold medals in a single Olympic Games. He also set an American record in the 100-yard butterfly at the AAU Indoor Championship in 1967.

ANSWER #38: C) WILMA RUDOLPH

Wilma Rudolph, an American sprinter, won gold in the 100m, 200m, and 4x100m relay at the 1960 Rome Olympics, earning the title "The Fastest Woman Alive."

ANSWER #39: C) LIVER

The first liver transplant was performed on March 1, 1963, by Dr. Thomas Starzl, known as "the father of modern transplantation." Unfortunately, the three-year-old patient did not survive the surgery due to complications.

ANSWER #40: C) TANG

Tang is a mixed brand drink that was formulated by William A. Mitchell and William James of General Foods Corporation. NASA selected the drink for use on John Glenn's 1962 Mercury flight and subsequent missions.

ANSWER #41: B) MADELEINE L 'ENGLE

A Wrinkle in Time, written by Madeleine L'Engle and published in 1962, won the 1963 Newbery Medal for best American children's book. The novel follows teenager Meg on a journey to rescue her father.

ANSWER #42: A) SAZERAC COCKTAIL

The Sazerac cocktail, made with cognac or whiskey, originated in New Orleans. It gained popularity in the 1960s when a French-owned family company began distributing it to local bars, often called coffee houses.

ANSWER #43: C) 1963

The P7 model oven introduced a pyrolytic cleaning method, where the oven heats to a high temperature to burn off debris. Once cooled, the ash can be easily wiped away.

ANSWER #44: B) STEVE MCQUEEN

Steve McQueen, a prominent actor in the 1960s and 1970s, gained fame for his role as a detective in the 1968 film *Bullitt*. Known for his "King of Cool" persona, he became an icon of the counterculture era.

ANSWER #45: D) 1963

Chevrolet debuted the second generation Corvette, modeled after the Stingray race car. By 1965, the Corvette featured a powerful Big Block V8 engine, generating 425 horsepower.

ANSWER #46: B) 1960

The oral polio vaccine is the most common type of vaccine that is used to fight polio. In 1960, an orally administered polio vaccine, developed by medical researcher Albert Sabin was introduced in the U.S. It was commercially used for the first time in 1961.

ANSWER #47: A) BEWITCHED

Bewitched was an American sitcom that aired from 1964 to 1972. The show starred Elizabeth Montgomery as Samantha, a suburban housewife who also happened to be a witch.

ANSWER #48: B) JOHN GLENN

John H. Glenn was the first American to orbit Earth on February 20, 1962, aboard "Friendship 7." He completed three orbits before safely landing after about five hours.

ANSWER #49: B) MURRAY THE K

Murray Kaufman, known as Murray the K, was a prominent NYC disc jockey. He gained fame in 1964 when The Beatles welcomed him into their circle after hearing about his influence from other musicians.

ANSWER #50: B) 1968

In 1968, AT&T proposed 911 as the national emergency number due to its simplicity. The first 911 call was made on February 16, 1968, by the Speaker of the Alabama House. Today, 911 remains the emergency number across the U.S.

ANSWER #51: B) MISTER MAGOO

The Pink Panther Show was a collection of cartoon shows that premiered in

1969. The show featured the panther, the inspector, and the cartoon cat all connected via a bumper sequence. The show also included an off-camera narrator called Marvin Miller.

ANSWER #52: A) RUDI GERNREICH

Rudi Gernreich was an American fashion designer known for his groundbreaking work in knitwear and swimsuits. He became internationally famous in 1964 for creating the topless "monokini."

ANSWER #53: D) SIDNEY POITIER

Sidney Poitier made history as the first Black actor to win an Academy Award for Best Actor, for his role in *Lilies of the Field* (1963). He also helped advance representation of Black actors in Hollywood by rejecting roles based on racial stereotypes.

ANSWER #54: A) MILTON BRADLEY

Milton Bradley created the 1962 edition of Candy Land, originally designed by Eleanor Abbott in 1949. The 1962 version featured a new track layout, solidifying its place as a classic board game.

ANSWER #55: C) POLLYANNA

Pollyanna (1960) starred Hayley Mills as a cheerful orphan who transforms a small town's outlook. Directed by David Swift, the film is based on Eleanor Porter's 1913 novel.

ANSWER #56: C) THE MONSTER MASH

The Monster Mash is a 1962 Halloween song by Bobby Pickett and the Crypt-Kickers, which inspired a popular dance of the same name. The song topped the Billboard chart during Halloween in 1973.

ANSWER #57: B) 1967

The first Super Bowl, held on January 15, 1967, at the Los Angeles Coliseum, was watched by over 65 million Americans. The Green Bay Packers, coached by Vince Lombardi, defeated the Kansas City Chiefs, coached by Hank Stram.

ANSWER #58: A) JOHN HUSTON

The Bible: In the Beginning... is a religious film released in 1966, directed by John Huston and produced by Dino De Laurentiis. The film narrates the first 22 chapters of the Book of Genesis, covering stories from the creation of Adam and Eve to the binding of Isaac.

ANSWER #59: C) ROWAN AND MARTIN'S LAUGH-IN

The phrase "you bet your sweet bippy" became popular on *Rowan and Martin's Laugh-In,* which aired from January 1968 to March 1973. The show introduced and popularized this playful expression.

ANSWER #60: B) BARRY GOLDWATER

Barry Goldwater, a U.S. Senator from Arizona, ran for President in 1964 as the Republican nominee. He lost to the incumbent, President Lyndon B. Johnson.

ANSWER #61: D) CHUBBY CHECKER

Chubby Checker created the Pony dance in the 1960s, where dancers mimic riding a pony with a prancing triple step. The dance was inspired by his hit song "The Pony Time."

ANSWER #62: D) 1965

Malcolm X, a civil rights activist, had his life story chronicled in *The*

Autobiography of Malcolm X, written by Alex Haley and published in 1965. The book details his journey from childhood to his activism.

ANSWER #63: A) DICK BIONDI

Dick Biondi, a renowned radio personality and DJ, was famous for his fast-talking style and earned nicknames like "The Screamer" and "The Wild Italian." His energetic persona made him a standout figure in radio.

ANSWER #64: C) LINCOLN CONTINENTAL

The Lincoln Continental is an American-made car that was first made in 1939. From 1961 to 1976, Lincoln sold the Continental as its exclusive model line. The fourth Generation of the Lincoln Continental was produced from 1961 to 1969.

ANSWER #65: D) THE FLINTSTONES

The Flintstones, which debuted on September 30, 1960, was the first original animated series to air in primetime. It held the record as the longest-running primetime cartoon until *The Simpsons* surpassed it in 1997.

ANSWER #66: B) 1968

On February 29, 1968, the White House hosted its first and only fashion show, organized by Lady Bird Johnson. Titled "How to Discover America in Style," the event aimed to celebrate American fashion and design while also promoting tourism and industry.

ANSWER #67: D) JOE WEATHERLY

Joe Weatherly began his car racing career in 1950. He was nicknamed "The Clown Prince of Stock Car Racing". Joe Weatherly won his first NASCAR

Premier Series championship in 1962 and a second championship the following year.

ANSWER #68: C) BATUSI

Batusi was a 1960s dance that was invented for use in the *Batman* television series. It was performed by Batman after being drugged by Molly. The dance involves making a horizontal V sign using one index and middle finger of both hands.

ANSWER #69: D) NASA

NASA launched its first weather satellite, TIROS-1, on April 1, 1960, to transmit atmospheric data to ground stations. Despite operating for just 78 days, it was a major success in space exploration.

ANSWER #70: D) NEW YORK

The first ATM in the U.S. was installed at Chemical Bank in Rockville Centre, New York, on September 2, 1969, following its invention by Fred J. Gentile and Wu Chang.

ANSWER #71: D) KIRK DOUGLAS

The Apartment is a 1960 comedy directed by Billy Wilder, starring Jack Lemmon, Fred MacMurray, Shirley MacLaine, and Ray Walston. It is widely considered one of the greatest films in history.

ANSWER #71: D) THE REIVERS

William Faulkner, who passed away in 1962 at the age of 64, was an acclaimed American novelist and Nobel Prize winner in Literature in 1949. His 19th novel, The Reivers, was published posthumously in June 1962.

ANSWER #73: C) HAROLD ROBBINS

The novel *The Adventurer* by Harold Robbins, published in 1966, tells a story of revolution and danger set in the jungles of South America. It was adapted into a film of the same name, released in 1970, and directed and produced by Lewis Gilbert.

ANSWER #74: D) 1968

Headache is a board game introduced in 1968 by the Kohner Brothers and later manufactured by Milton Bradley. The objective is to land a playing piece, called "cones," on top of all opponents' pieces, with 2 to 4 players participating.

ANSWER #75: C) A CHARLIE BROWN CHRISTMAS

"A Charlie Brown Christmas" aired in 1965 as the first animated TV special by Charles M. Schulz and Bill Melendez. It quickly became a beloved holiday classic, featuring the Peanuts gang and a memorable jazz score by Vince Guaraldi.

1970s Questions

#1 - WHICH FEMALE TENNIS STAR FACED BOBBY RIGGS IN THE "BATTLE OF THE SEXES?"

A) Billie Jean King

C) Margaret Court

B) Chris Evert

D) Tracy Austin

#2 ~ IN WHICH YEAR WAS THE "Y.M.C.A" DANCE SONG RELEASED?

A) 1970

C) 1975

B) 1978

D) 1976

#3 - UNDER WHICH U.S. PRESIDENT DID THE IRANIAN HOSTAGE CRISIS TAKE PLACE?

A) Jimmy Carter

C) Ronald Reagan

B) Richard Nixon

D) Bill Clinton

#4 - THE SLANG "GOOF" WAS USED TO DESCRIBE WHAT TYPE OF PERSON?

A) Skinny

C) Annoying

B) Silly

D) Big

#5 - WHICH YEAR DID THE LEGENDARY ELVIS PRESLEY DIE?

A) 1970

C) 1977

B) 1972

D) 1979

#6 - WHICH YEAR WAS *SOPHIE'S CHOICE* PUBLISHED?

A) 1971

C) 1970

B) 1979

D) 1975

#7 - WHO INVENTED THE FIRST CELL PHONE IN 1973?

A) Martin Cooper

C) Orville Wright

B) Thomas Edison

D) Frederick Jones

#8 - FROM WHICH FILM DID THE 1976 TELEVISION SERIES *THE BIONIC WOMAN* ORIGINATE AS A SPINOFF?

A) Adam-12

C) The Love Boat

B) Quincy, M.E

D) The Six Million Dollar Man

#9 - WHICH OF THE FOLLOWING PLAYED A ROLE IN THE 1970S FILM *LITTLE BIG MAN*?

A) Jack Nicholson

C) Dustin Hoffman

B) Robert Redford

D) Paul Newman

#10 - WHO WAS THE FIRST BOXER TO DEFEAT THE LEGENDARY MUHAMMAD ALI?

A) Larry Holmes

C) Robert Duran

B) George Foreman

D) Joe Frazier

#11 - WHICH 1970S MOVIE WAS BASED ON THE REAL HISTORY OF CALIFORNIA'S "WATER WARS"?

A) Star Wars

C) Taxi Driver

B) Jaws

D) Chinatown

#12 - WHICH OF THIS 1970S SLANG WAS USED TO DESCRIBE GOING CRAZY?

A) Tripping

C) Go bananas

B) Right on

D) Bugged out

#13 - WHICH 1970S GOLFER IS NICKNAMED "TOWERING INFERNO"?

A) Tom Weiskopf

C) Tommy Aaron

B) Andy North

D) Lou Graham

#14 - WHICH FOOTBALL PLAYER WAS KNOWN AS "CAPTAIN AMERICA?"

A) Terry Bradshaw

C) Bob Lilly

B) Roger Staubach

D) Joe Greene

#15 - IN WHICH YEAR WAS THE RUBIK'S CUBE INVENTED?

A) 1970

C) 1974

B) 1978

D) 1979

#16 - WHICH 1970S SLANG WAS MADE FAMOUS IN THE 1975 SONG "CONVOY?"

A) Keep on truckin'

C) Boogie

B) Stick it to the Man

D) 10-4

#17 - WHICH AUTHOR WROTE *THE BLUEST EYE*, PUBLISHED IN 1970?

A) Gloria Steinem

C) Dawnie Walton

B) Toni Morrison

D) Taylor Reid

#18 - WHAT U.S. DEPARTMENT WAS RESPONSIBLE FOR THE DEVELOPMENT OF GPS?

A) U.S. Department of Finance

C) U.S. Department of Housing

B) U.S. Department of Defence

D) U.S. Department of Education

#19 - WHO CREATED THE FAMOUS "COOKIE DIET" IN THE 1970S

A) Jane Fonda

C) Richard Simmons

B) Daniel Abraham

D) Dr. Sanford Siegal

#20 - HOW MANY SEASONS DID THE 1970S SERIES *BONANZA* HAVE?

A) 18

C) 14

B) 9

D) 20

#21 - WHICH OF THE FOLLOWING WARS ENDED IN 1975?

A) Korean War

C) Civil War

B) Iraq War

D) Vietnam War

#22 - WHICH OF THESE WAS NOT A MUHAMMAD ALI MATCH?

A) The Thrilla in Manilla

C) The Brawl in Montreal

B) Rumble in the Jungle

D) The Fight of the Century

#23 - WHICH OF THESE IS NOT ONE OF STEPHEN KING'S BOOKS OF THE 1970S?

A) Trinity

C) Salem's lot

B) Carrie

D) The Shining

#24 - IN WHICH 1970S FILM DID SYLVESTER STALLONE PLAY A DEBT COLLECTOR TURNED BOXER?

A) Chinatown

C) Alien

B) Rocky

D) Jaws

#25 - WHAT EXPRESSION WOULD YOU USE TO TELL SOMEONE TO STAY OUT OF YOUR BUSINESS?

A) "Stop dipping in my Kool-Aid"

C) "Wally wally, blood and dolly"

B) "Up your nose with a rubber hose"

D) "You ain't just a woofin"

#26 - WHO PLAYED THE ROLE OF "WONDER WOMAN" IN THE 1970S TV SERIES?

A) Karen Grassle

C) Lynda Carter

B) Melissa Sue

D) Shirley Feeney

#27 - THE 1970S WRAP DRESSES WERE INTRODUCED BY WHICH OF THE FOLLOWING DESIGNERS?

A) Diane von Furstenberg

C) Thea Porter

B) Bill Gibb

D) Jeriana San Juan

#28 - WHICH 1970S NBA PLAYER WAS AWARDED THE 2016 PRESIDENTIAL MEDAL OF FREEDOM?

A) Walt Frazier

C) Kareem Abdul-Jabbar

B) Pete Maravich

D) Bill Walton

#29 - THE FIRST SELF-CONTAINED DIGITAL CAMERA WAS INVENTED BY WHO?

A) Steve Sasson

C) Ted Hoff

B) Ray Tomlinson

D) Stanley Mazor

#30 - WHO WROTE THE FAMOUS BOOK *FEAR OF FLYING*?

A) Taylor Jenkin

C) Erica Jong

B) Irving Stone

D) Ann Rice

#31 - WHO PLAYED THE ROLE OF PRIVATE DETECTIVE JAKE GITTES IN THE 1974 FILM *CHINATOWN*?

A) Robert Redford

C) Robert De Niro

B) Dustin Hoffman

D) Jack Nicholson

#32 - WHICH OF THESE FILMS IS BASED ON PRESIDENT NIXON AND THE WATERGATE SCANDAL?

A) All the President's Men

C) The American President

B) The Butler

D) Thirteen Days

#33 - WHO PLAYED THE TITLE CHARACTER OF THE 1978 FILM *SUPERMAN*?

A) Harrison Ford

B) Christopher Reeve

C) David Carradine

D) Donald Sutherland

#34 - WHAT 1970S EXPRESSION MEANS TO GET RID OF SOMETHING?

A) Deep Six

C) 10-4

B) Guilt Trip

D) Burnout

#35 - WHO INVENTED EMAIL IN 1971?

A) Warren L. Dalziel

C) Steve Wozniak

B) Terry Walker

D) Ray Tomlinson

#36 - WHICH OF THESE BOOKS IS BASED ON BENJAMIN HOOK'S *IT WAS THE STORY OF OUR PEOPLE*?

A) Fear of Flying

C) The Rachel Papers

B) Gravity's Rainbow

D) Roots

#37 - WHICH FILM WON THE 1979 ACADEMY AWARD FOR BEST ART DIRECTION?

A) Heaven Can Wait   C) Sleuth

B) Film Night   D) The French Connection

#38 - WHICH U.S. PRESIDENT WAS THE FIRST TO VISIT CHINA?

A) George Bush   C) Richard Nixon

B) Jimmy Carter   D) Ronald Reagan

#39 - WHICH ARTIST SANG THE 1978S SONG "I WILL SURVIVE"?

A) Debby Boone   C) Andy Gibb

B) Gloria Gaynor   D) Marvin Gaye

#40 - WHICH RADIO PERSONALITY WAS KNOWN AS THE "ACE FROM OUTER SPACE"?

A) Wolfman Jack   C) Jocko Henderson

B) Casey Kasem   D) Ryan Seacrest

#41- WHAT 1970'S DANCE WAS ALSO KNOWN AS "THE MANNEQUIN"?

A) YMCA dance   C) The Robot

B) The Disco Finger   D) The Bus Stop

#42 - WHO WAS VICE PRESIDENT UNDER PRESIDENT JIMMY CARTER?

A) Walter Mondale

C) George H. Bush

B) George Busbeee

D) Dan Quayle

#43 - WHICH '70S CAR WAS NICKNAMED "THE FLYING FISHBOWL"?

A) 1973 Pontiac Grand Am

C) 1976 Dodge Aspen

B) 1971 Chevrolet Vega

D) 1975 AMC Pacer

#44 - WHICH OF THESE WAS A SPIN-OFF OF THE 1970S SHOW *ALL IN THE FAMILY*?

A) Columbo

C) The Jeffersons

B) Happy Days

D) The Incredible Hulk

#45 - WHICH OF THESE IS A MICHAEL JACKSON 1970S SONG?

A) Love Train

C) Night Fever

B) Don't Stop Til You Get Enough

D) Dreams

#46 - WHICH U.S. VICE PRESIDENT RESIGNED FROM OFFICE IN 1973?

A) George Bush

C) Dick Cheney

B) Walter Mondale

D) Spiro Agnew

#47 - WHICH ACTOR STARRED IN THE 1973 FILM *THE EXORCIST*?

A) Ellen Burstyn   C) Pam Grier

B) Jayne Kennedy   D) Olivia Newton-John

#48 - WHICH OF THE FOLLOWING ACTORS WAS AWARDED A STAR ON THE HOLLYWOOD WALK OF FAME IN 1977?

A) Robert Redford   C) Denzel Washington

B) Al Pacino   D) Jack Albertson

#49 - WHICH ARTIST IS CREDITED WITH THE FAMOUS 1970S DANCE "THE HUSTLE"?

A) Marvin Gaye   C) Don McLean

B) Van McCoy   D) Rod Stewart

#50 - IN WHICH YEAR WAS THE "STAY ALIVE" BOARD GAME RELEASED?

A) 1978   C) 1974

B) 1979   D) 1971

#51 - WHICH ICONIC ROCK BAND RELEASED THE ALBUM "THE DARK SIDE OF THE MOON" IN 1973?

A) Pink Floyd   C) The Rolling Stones

B) Led Zeppelin   D) The Who

#52 - WHICH OF THESE WAS FORD'S FIRST SUBCOMPACT CAR IN NORTH AMERICA?

A) 1971 Ford Pinto

C) 1977 Ford LTD II

B) 1975 Ford Ranger

D) 1976 Ford Mustang

#53 - WHO WAS THE FIRST WOMAN TO RECEIVE THE BILLBOARD AWARD FOR FM PERSONALITY OF THE YEAR?

A) Alison Steele

C) Elsie Janis

B) Lisa Glasberg

D) Anne Hummert

#54 - WHICH DANCE WAS MADE FAMOUS BY THE FILM *SATURDAY NIGHT FEVER*?

A) The Funky Chicken Dance

C) YMCA Dance

B) The Disco Finger

D) The Bump

#55 - WHICH BOARD GAME WAS DESIGNED BY GARY GYGAX AND DAVE ARNESON?

A) Dungeons and Dragons

C) Trouble

B) Monopoly

D) Backgammon

#56 - WHICH OF THE FOLLOWING ACTORS STARRED IN THE 1976 FILM *TAXI DRIVER*?

A) Marlo Brando

C) David Carradine

B) Robert De Niro

D) Harrison Ford

#57 - WHICH AMERICAN ACTRESS POPULARIZED THE ONE-PIECE SWIMSUIT?

A) Shelley Hack

C) Jane Fonda

B) Jayne Kennedy

D) Farrah Fawcett

#58 - BESIDES KATE BLOOMBERG, WHO ELSE PARTICIPATED IN THE INVENTION OF THE SHRINKY DINKS?

A) Betty Morris

C) Morrison Michtom

B) Louis Marx

D) Helen Herrick Malsed

#59 - WHICH YEAR DID THE AMERICAN BASKETBALL ASSOCIATION (ABA) CEASE OPERATIONS?

A) 1971

C) 1976

B) 1969

D) 1978

#60 - WHO CREATED THE DEXATRIM APPETITE SUPPRESSANT?

A) S. Daniel Abraham

C) Richard Simmons

B) Dr. Sanford Siegal

D) Robert Atkins

#61 - WHICH OF THESE WAS THE FIRST EVER HOME VIDEO GAME IN NORTH AMERICA?

A) Galaxy

C) Pong

B) The Odyssey

D) The Oregon

#62 - WHICH TOY WAS INVENTED BY PILOT CORPORATION IN 1974?

A) Rubik's Cube

C) Magna Doodles

B) Playmobil

D) Pay Day

#63 - WHICH DESIGNER CAME UP WITH THE BOGGLE GAME?

A) Dave Arneson

C) Don Daglow

B) Allan Turoff

D) Toby Gard

#64 - 1977 FILM *SUSPIRIA* STARRED WHICH OF THE FOLLOWING ACTRESSES?

A) Pam Grier

C) Jayne Kennedy

B) Shelley Hack

D) Jessica Harper

#65 - WHICH AMERICAN ENGINEER INVENTED THE CUISINART FOOD PROCESSOR?

A) Henry Shull Arms

C) James Albus

B) Carl Sontheimer

D) Amos Wilnai

#66 - WHICH RADIO PERSONALITY VOICED SHAGGY IN *SCOOBY-DOO*?

A) Ryan Seacrest

C) Casey Kasem

B) Howard Stern

D) Robert Morgan

#67 - WHAT WAS THE NAME OF THE FIRST EVER DIGITAL ELECTRIC WATCH?

A) The Pulsar   C) Omega

B) Cartier   D) Hublot

#68 - IN WHICH YEAR WAS JOHN PAUL II ELECTED AS POPE?

A) 1970   C) 1971

B) 1974   D) 1978

#69 - WHICH OF THE FOLLOWING WAS NOT A MAIN CAST MEMBER OF THE 1970S SHOW *CHARLIE'S ANGELS*?

A) Kate Jackson   C) Jaclyn Smith

B) Farrah Fawcett   D) Lynda Carter

#70 - WHO POPULARIZED THE CIRCULAR SUNGLASSES?

A) John Lennon   C) Stevie Wonder

B) Diana Ross   D) Willie Nelson

#71 - WHICH SALAD WAS ORIGINALLY KNOWN AS "PISTACHIO PINEAPPLE DELIGHT"?

A) Watergate Salad   C) Taco Salad

B) Chopped Power Salad   D) Caesar Salad

#72 - WHICH LEAGUE MERGED WITH THE NFL IN 1970?

A) National Arena League

C) United Football League

B) American Football League

D) The XFL

#73 - WHO STARRED IN THE 1975 FILM *NASHVILLE*?

A) Faye Dunaway

C) Richard Harris

B) Lily Tomlin

D) Diane Keaton

#74 - IN WHICH YEAR WAS THE COOKER REINTRODUCED AS THE CROCK-POT?

A) 1971

C) 1970

B) 1977

D) 1979

#75 - IN WHICH YEAR WAS THE RADIO SHOW *ALL THINGS CONSIDERED* LAUNCHED?

A) 1968

C) 1985

B) 1971

D) 1979

1970s: Answer Key

ANSWER #1: A) BILLIE JEAN KING

The Battle of the Sexes was a famous tennis match on September 20, 1973, where Billie Jean King defeated former men's champion Bobby Riggs, who had boasted he could beat any female player.

ANSWER #2: B) 1978

"Y.M.C.A," a 1978 hit by the Village People, features a dance where arm movements form the letters "Y," "M," "C," and "A."

ANSWER #3: A) JIMMY CARTER

On November 4, 1979, Iranian students took 66 Americans hostage in the U.S. Embassy in Tehran, with 52 held for over a year. The crisis occurred during Jimmy Carter's presidency and ended shortly after Ronald Reagan took office.

ANSWER #4: B) SILLY

The 1970s introduced unique slang, with some terms like "silly" persisting, while others faded with the era.

ANSWER #5: C) 1977

Elvis Presley, a famous rock singer known as the "King of Rock and Roll," tragically died on August 16, 1977, at his Memphis home. His death was linked to years of prescription drug abuse and unhealthy eating habits.

ANSWER #6: B) 1979

Sophie's Choice, a 1979 novel by William Styron, was set in the 1940s, and tells the story and growth of a friendship between a young Southern writer and a Roman Catholic woman from Poland who survived the Nazi death camp.

ANSWER #7: A) MARTIN COOPER

On April 3, 1973, Martin Cooper made the first public cell phone call on a DynaTAC phone to Joel Engel of AT&T's rival project to test the device before the press conference.

ANSWER #8: D) THE SIX MILLION DOLLAR MAN

The Bionic Woman (1976-77) was a spin-off from *The Six Million Dollar Man*. Based on Martin Caidin's 1972 novel *Cyborg*, it starred Lindsay Wagner as Jamie Sommers.

ANSWER #9: C) DUSTIN HOFFMAN

Dustin Hoffman, known for his antihero roles, gained fame with his performance in the 1970 film *Little Big Man*. His role as a witness to the American genocide made him a 1970s icon.

ANSWER #10: D) JOE FRAZIER

The match, known as the "Fight of the Century," took place on March 8, 1971, at Madison Square Garden in New York. In this iconic bout, Joe Frazier handed Muhammad Ali his first loss by unanimous decision.

ANSWER #11: D) CHINATOWN

Chinatown delves into the California Water Wars, showcasing the corruption behind Los Angeles's growth. Acclaimed for its realistic depiction of crime and politics, the film highlights the murky intersection of business and corruption.

ANSWER #12: C) GO BANANAS

"Go bananas," an extremely popular 1970s slang term that was primarily used by young people, described someone acting crazy or insane. Interestingly, the phrase remains in use today.

ANSWER #13: A) TOM WEISKOPF

Tom Weiskopf, a standout golfer in the 1960s and '70s, won the 1973 Open Championship. Nicknamed "Towering Inferno" for his height and temper, he also had five runner-up finishes in majors.

ANSWER #14: B) ROBERT STAUBACH

Roger Staubach is a retired American football quarterback who was key in the success of the Dallas Cowboys in the 1970s. He is known as "Captain Comeback."

ANSWER #15: C) 1974

Invented by Hungarian architect Erno Rubik in 1974, the Rubik's Cube was initially called the "Buvos Kocka" or "Magic Cube." Rubik created it to demonstrate 3D movement to his students.

ANSWER #16: D) 10-4

The slang "10-4" comes from 1930s police radio codes, meaning "message received." Adopted by truck drivers and popularized by the song "Convoy" by W. McCall, it's akin to saying "Roger that."

ANSWER #17: B) TONI MORRISON

Toni Morrison's debut novel, *The Bluest Eye* (1970), follows Pecola, a young Black girl battling low self-esteem. Morrison's impactful storytelling later earned her a Pulitzer Prize.

ANSWER #18: B) U.S DEPARTMENT OF DEFENSE

In the early 1970s, the U.S. Department of Defense developed the NAVSTAR satellite, launched in 1978, which evolved into today's GPS system.

ANSWER #19: D) DR. SANFORD SIEGAL

Dr. Sanford Siegal created the cookie diet in the 1970s, replacing meals with cookies formulated to control hunger through a unique blend of amino acids.

ANSWER #20: C) 14

Bonanza, which aired from 1959 to 1973, is the second longest-running western series, following *Gunsmoke*. It chronicles the lives of a ranching family in Nevada.

ANSWER #21: D) VIETNAM WAR

The Vietnam War, starting in the late 1950s, was fought between communist North Vietnam and South Vietnam, supported by the U.S. It ended on April 30, 1975, when North Vietnamese tanks entered Saigon.

ANSWER #22: C) THE BRAWL IN MONTREAL

"The Rumble in the Jungle" was a bout between Ali and George Foreman, held on October 30, 1974. "The Thrilla in Manila" was the third fight between Ali and Joe Frazier, taking place on October 1, 1975, in Manila, Philippines. "The Fight of the Century" was another legendary match between Ali and Frazier, occurring on March 8, 1971.

ANSWER #23: A) TRINITY

Stephen King's first novel, *Carrie* (1974), is about a tormented girl with telekinetic powers. He followed with *Salem's Lot* (1975) and *The Shining* (1977), adapted into a film in 1980.

ANSWER #24: B) ROCKY

Rocky was the highest-grossing film of 1976, earning over $117 million. It received 10 Academy Award nominations and won three. Sylvester Stallone wrote the script in three days.

ANSWER #25: A) STOP DIPPING IN MY KOOL-AID

The expression "stop dipping in my Kool-Aid" meant somebody getting all up into someone's business and getting things wrong.

ANSWER #26: C) LYNDA CARTER

Lynda Carter is an American singer and actress best known for her role as the star of the television series *Wonder Woman*, based on the DC comic book superhero of the same name. The show aired from 1975 to 1979.

ANSWER #27: A) DIANE VON FURSTENBERG

The wrap dress, designed by renowned fashion designer Diane von Furstenberg in 1974, is a celebrated garment known for its distinctive style.

ANSWER #28: C) KAREEM ABDUL-JABBAR

Kareem Abdul-Jabbar was an NBA player who dominated basketball in the 1970s and 1980s. Kareem broke several records such as becoming a six-time MVP for the league. He was also voted MVP for a record six times.

ANSWER #29: A) STEVE SASSON

In 1975, Steve Sasson invented the first self-contained digital camera while working for Eastman Kodak in New York. This digital camera could only capture black-and-white images, which were stored on a digital cassette tape.

ANSWER #30: C) ERICA JONG

Erica Jong's 1973 novel *Fear of Flying* follows Isadora Wing's quest for freedom and explores women's roles and sexuality. The book stirred controversy for its frank depiction of female desire.

ANSWER #31: D) JACK NICHOLSON

Jack Nicholson gained major recognition with *Easy Rider* (1969) and solidified his fame with *Chinatown* (1974), directed by Roman Polanski and written by Robert Towne.

ANSWER #32: A) ALL THE PRESIDENT'S MEN

All the President's Men was released in July 1976. The film is an adaptation of Bob Woodward and Carl Bernstein's best-selling book, and depicts the Watergate Scandal that took place during the administration of President Richard Nixon.

Answer #33: B) CHRISTOPHER REEVE

Christopher Reeve became famous as Superman in 1978 and starred in three sequels. In 1995, a fall from a horse left him quadriplegic.

ANSWER #34: A) DEEP SIX

"Deep-Six," originally 1920s slang for a grave, resurfaced in the 1970s meaning "getting rid of something." It gained popularity during the Watergate Scandal to describe the cover-up.

ANSWER #35: D) RAY TOMLINSON

Ray Tomlinson invented email in 1971 while working on ARPANET. He developed a program that enabled message exchange between computers on the network.

ANSWER #36: D) ROOTS

Roots, a 1976 novel by Alex Haley, traces Kunta Kinte's abduction from Africa and his life as a slave in Virginia.

ANSWER #37: A) HEAVEN CAN WAIT

Heaven Can Wait (1978) is about a young man mistakenly sent to heaven by his guardian angel. The film was nominated for nine Academy Awards and won one for Best Art Direction.

ANSWER #38: C) RICHARD NIXON

Richard Nixon, the 37th U.S. President, became the first to visit China on February 21, 1972. His visit was a key moment in establishing diplomatic relations between the two nations.

ANSWER #39: B) GLORIA GAYNOR

Gloria Gaynor's disco hit "I Will Survive," released in October 1978, captures her strength after a breakup. Written by Dino Fekaris and Freddie Perren, it won the Grammy for Best Disco Recording in 1980.

ANSWER #40: C) JOCKO HENDERSON

Jocko Henderson, a prominent hip-hop and radio personality in Baltimore and New York, was known as the biggest Black DJ of his era. His fans nicknamed him "Ace from Outer Space."

ANSWER #41: C) THE ROBOT

The Robot, also known as "The Mannequin" or "The Dancing Machine," is a 1970s dance mimicking robot-like movements. Michael Jackson popularized it with his brothers.

ANSWER #42: A) WALTER MONDALE

Jimmy Carter served as the 39th President of the United States. He was elected President in 1977 and only served one term up to 1981. His Vice President was Walter Mondale who served as the 42nd Vice President of The United States.

ANSWER #43: D) 1975 AMC PACER

The 1975 AMC Pacer, known as "The Flying Fishbowl" for its distinctive rear window design, was the first modern American car mass-produced with a cab-forward concept.

ANSWER #44: C) THE JEFFERSONS

The Jeffersons, an American sitcom airing from 1975 to 1985, had 253 episodes and one spin-off, *Checking In*. The series ended abruptly without a finale.

ANSWER #45: B) DON'T STOP TIL YOU GET ENOUGH

Released on July 10, 1979, Michael Jackson's "Don't Stop 'Til You Get Enough" was the lead track on his album *Off the Wall*. The song earned Platinum certification in the U.S.

ANSWER #46: D) SPIRO AGNEW

Spiro Agnew, the 39th U.S. Vice President (1969-1973), resigned on October 10, 1973, amid bribery and extortion investigations. He was only the second VP to resign, after John Calhoun in 1832.

ANSWER #47: A) ELLEN BURSTYN

The Exorcist (1973), directed by William Friedkin and written by William Peter Blatty, starred Ellen Burstyn, Max von Sydow, and Linda Blair. It's an adaptation of Blatty's novel.

ANSWER 48: D) JACK ALBERTSON

Jack Albertson, an American singer, dancer, and actor, received a star on the Hollywood Walk of Fame in 1977.

ANSWER #49: B) VAN MCCOY

"The Hustle," a 1970s dance popularized by Van McCoy's 1975 hit song of the same name, involves four basic moves: stepping, the chicken dance, twirling, and turning.

ANSWER #50: D) 1971

"Stay Alive", a board game by Milton Bradley where players protect marbles from falling through holes, was released in 1971.

ANSWER #51: A) PINK FLOYD

Pink Floyd's *The Dark Side of the Moon* (1973) is a landmark album renowned for its studio effects and philosophical lyrics. It set a record by staying on the Billboard charts for 741 weeks, solidifying Pink Floyd's place in rock history.

ANSWER #52: A) 1971 FORD PINTO

The 1971 Ford Pinto was Ford's first subcompact model in North America, with over three million units produced.

ANSWER #53: A) ALISON STEELE

Alison Steele, known as "The Nightbird," was a pioneering radio personality honored with the Billboard Award for FM Personality of the Year in 1976. The Alison Steele Award for Lifetime Achievement was named in her honor.

ANSWER #54: B) THE DISCO FINGER

The Disco Finger Dance, popularized by John Travolta in *Saturday Night*

Fever, is a 1970s move involving extending the index finger and moving it up and down diagonally while swaying the hips.

ANSWER #55: A) DUNGEONS AND DRAGONS

Dungeons and Dragons, first published in 1974, became a national sensation by allowing players to create and control their own characters.

ANSWER 56: B) ROBERT DE NIRO

Taxi Driver (1976), written by Paul Schrader and directed by Martin Scorsese, stars Robert De Niro as the troubled Travis Bickle. It is renowned as one of the greatest and most controversial films in history.

ANSWER #57: D) FARRAH FAWCETT

The one-piece swimsuit, first designed in the early 20th century, surged in popularity in 1977 when American actress Farrah Fawcett wore it, making it a major fashion trend of the decade.

ANSWER #58: A) BETTY MORRIS

Shrinky Dinks, a toy made from polystyrene sheets, was invented in 1973 by Betty Morris and Kate Bloomberg. It was later licensed to major toy manufacturers like Milton Bradley.

ANSWER #59: C) 1976

The American Basketball Association (ABA), active from 1967 to 1976, merged with the NBA in 1976. The New York Nets won the final ABA championship, marking the league's end.

ANSWER #60: A) S. DANIEL ABRAHAM

Dexatrim, a popular 1970s weight loss supplement, contains

phenylpropanolamine, typically used for allergies. It was designed to assist in weight control.

ANSWER #61: B) THE ODYSSEY

Released by Magnavox in September 1972, *The Odyssey* was one of the first home video game consoles. It featured a box with black, white, and brown colors, connected to a TV with wired controllers.

ANSWER #62: C) MAGNA DOODLES

Magna Doodles, a magnetic drawing toy, was invented by the Pilot Corporation in 1974. It became trademarked in the U.S. in 1986.

ANSWER #63: B) ALLAN TUROFF

Boggle, a word game where players find words in a grid of lettered dice, was published in 1972 by Parker Brothers. It can be played solo or with others.

ANSWER #64: D) JESSICA HARPER

Suspiria (1977), directed by Dario Argento, stars Jessica Harper as an American ballet student at a prestigious academy. The film is renowned for its influence in the horror genre.

ANSWER #65: B) CARL SONTHEIMER

Carl Sontheimer invented the Cuisinart food processor in 1973, based on a French commercial model. He also developed other kitchen appliances and a microwave-based direction finder used in NASA's moon landing.

ANSWER #66: C) CASEY KASEM

Casey Kasem, known for his voice work, hosted *America's Top 40* from 1970 to 1988. He also voiced "Shaggy" in *Scooby-Doo* and had a notable career in radio and animation.

ANSWER #67: A) THE PULSAR

The Pulsar, unveiled on May 5, 1970, on *The Tonight Show* by Johnny Carson, was the first digital electric watch. It used LEDs to display time and had no moving parts.

ANSWER #68: D) 1978

John Paul II became Pope on October 16, 1978, making him the first non-Italian pope elected since 1523. He served until his death on April 2, 2005, and was the second-longest-serving pope in history. His birth name was Karol Jozef Wojtyla.

ANSWER #69: D) LYNDA CARTER

Charlie's Angels aired from 1976 to 1981 and starred Kate Jackson, Jaclyn Smith, and Farrah Fawcett. Lynda Carter, known for Wonder Woman, was not in the show.

ANSWER #70: A) JOHN LENNON

John Lennon popularized circular sunglasses in the 1970s, making them a signature part of his style.

ANSWER #71: A) WATERGATE SALAD

Watergate salad, also known as Pistachio Pineapple Delight, is made from pistachio pudding, pecans, marshmallows, and canned pineapple. Its popularity surged during the Watergate scandal.

ANSWER #72: B) AMERICAN FOOTBALL LEAGUE

The American Football League (AFL) merged with the National Football League (NFL) in 1970. The merger included 10 AFL teams joining the NFL, which retained its name. Unified rules were adopted by the end of that year.

ANSWER #73: B) LILY TOMLIN

Nashville (1975), directed by Robert Altman, explores the lives of people in the country and gospel music scene in Nashville. The film features Lily Tomlin, David Arkin, and Barbara Baxley.

ANSWER #74: A) 1971

The crock-pot, a countertop appliance for simmering food at low temperatures, was initially called the cooker. It was renamed and reintroduced as the crock-pot in 1971.

ANSWER #75: B) 1971

All Things Considered is a news program launched on May 3, 1971, on NPR. It features news, commentary, analysis, segments, and interviews. Robert Conley was the program's first host.

1980s Questions

#1 - WHO WAS THE VICE PRESIDENT UNDER RONALD REAGAN?

A) Dan Quayle

C) Dick Cheney

B) Al Gore

D) George H. W. Bush

#2 - IN WHICH TELEVISION NETWORK DID THE ICONIC *THE COSBY SHOW* AIR?

A) CBS

C) ABC

B) NBC

D) HBO

#3 - WHO WAS APPOINTED THE FIRST FEMALE SUPREME COURT JUSTICE IN 1981?

A) Amy Coney Barrett

C) Sonia Sotomayor

B) Sandra Day O'Connor

D) Ruth Bader Ginsburg

#4 - WHICH FAMOUS GAME CONSOLE WAS HOME FOR THE GAME TETRIS?

A) Nintendo Game Boy

C) Super Pocket

B) Atari

D) PlayStation 1

#5 - WHICH 1980S NBA LEGEND IS NICKNAMED "MAGIC"?

A) Michael Jordan

C) Larry Bird

B) Earvin Johnson

D) Dennis Johnson

#6 - WHAT WAS THE FIRST CONSUMER-READY DISPOSABLE CAMERA CALLED?

A) The Fling

C) Sony Walkman

B) Sony Rolly

D) Camcorder

#7 - WHAT DID THE 1980S SLANG "BAD" MEAN?

A) Radical

C) Happy

B) Very good

D) Car

#8 - WHICH FAMOUS TOY COULD TURN FROM AN ACTION FIGURE INTO A CAR?

A) Transformer

C) Care Bears

B) Cabbage Patch Kids

D) My Little Pony

#9 - WHICH LIGHT AND STRETCHY MATERIAL BECAME AN INTEGRAL PART OF 1980S FASHION?

A) Muslin

C) Spandex

B) Chiffon

D) Denim

#10 - WHO SANG THE ICONIC SONG "PURPLE RAIN"?

A) Michael Jackson

C) Whitney Houston

B) Prince

D) Madonna

#11 - WHAT WAS THE NAME OF THE PORTABLE RADIO THAT BECAME ICONIC IN URBAN AREAS DURING THE 1980S FOR ITS ROLE IN PROVIDING A MOBILE SOUNDTRACK?

A) Home theater

C) Bluetooth speaker

B) Boombox

D) Earbuds

#12 - WHAT POPULAR 1980S HOUSEHOLD GADGET BECAME WIDELY USED FOR MAKING COFFEE AT HOME?

A) Coffee grinder

C) Coffee dripper

B) Espresso machine

D) Coffee roaster

#13 - WHICH 1980'S DANCE MOVE WAS POPULARIZED BY THE ICONIC SINGER MICHAEL JACKSON?

A) Moonwalk

C) The Cabbage Patch

B) Breakdancing

D) Running Man

#14 - WHO SANG THE FAMOUS SONG "DON'T WORRY BE HAPPY"?

A) Madonna

C) Steve Tyler

B) Kate Bush

D) Bobby McFerrin

#15 - WHAT 1980S TERM WAS USED TO REFER TO A LAZY PERSON WHO SPENDS MOST OF THEIR TIME SITTING AND WATCHING TV?

A) Couch Potato

C) Radical

B) Tubular

D) Grody

#16 - WHAT WAS THE NAME OF THE SPACE SHUTTLE THAT EXPLODED AFTER LIFTOFF IN 1986?

A) Discovery

C) Endeavour

B) Challenger

D) Atlantis

#17 - WHO WAS THE FIRST AMERICAN WOMAN TO GO TO SPACE IN 1983?

A) Amelia Earhart

C) Sally Ride

B) Geraldine "Jerrie" Mock

D) Valentina Tereshkova

#18 - WHAT YEAR WAS MICHAEL JACKSON'S "THRILLER" MUSIC VIDEO RELEASED?

A) 1984

C) 1989

B) 1987

D) 1983

#19 - ON WHICH RADIO STATION DID *THE HOWARD STERN SHOW* ORIGINALLY AIR?

A) WNBC

C) Sirius XM

B) WXRK-FM

D) WCCC

#20 - WHICH ICONIC 1980S CAR WAS DUBBED THE "FOX BODY"?

A) Audi Quattro

C) Porsche 959

B) Ford Mustang

D) Ford Sierra RS

#21 - WHAT SHOW DID SINGER AND ACTOR RICK SPRINGFIELD STAR IN 1981?

A) The Fall Guy

C) General Hospital

B) Dynasty

D) Hill Street Blues

#22 - WHICH FAMOUS 1980S DANCE MOVE WAS DERIVED FROM A FAMOUS CHILDREN'S TOY?

A) The Cabbage Patch

C) The Electric Slide

B) Footloose

D) The Robot

#23 - WHO WAS THE LEAD ACTOR IN THE 1981 MOVIE *CARBON COPY*?

A) Bill Murray   C) Jack Nicholson

B) Eddie Murphy   D) Denzel Washington

#24 - WHICH 1980'S BASEBALL PLAYER WAS NICKNAMED "THE KID"?

A) Wade Boggs   C) Eddie Murray

B) Dale Murphy   D) Ken Griffey Jr.

#25 - WHO WROTE THE BOOK *THE HANDMAID'S TALE* IN 1985?

A) Alan Moore   C) Anne Tyler

B) Isabel Allende   D) Margaret Atwood

#26 - WHICH ARTIST CREATED THE "WOP" DANCE?

A) J. Dash   C) Tone Loc

B) Eminem   D) LL Cool J

#27 - WHICH BAND SANG THE 1985 HIT "EVERYBODY WANTS TO RULE THE WORLD"?

A) Van Halen   C) Guns N' Roses

B) U2   D) Tears for Fears

#28 - WHICH CAR WAS RELEASED IN 1987 TO MARK FERRARI'S 40TH ANNIVERSARY?

A) Ferrari 308 GTSi

C) Ferrari F40

B) Ferrari 408 4RM

D) Ferrari 348 TB

#29 - HOW LONG DID IT TAKE JOHN HUGHES TO WRITE *FERRIS BUELLER'S DAY OFF*?

A) 6 months

C) 1 year

B) 6 days

D) 3 months

#30 - WHO WROTE THE ICONIC 1982 BOOK, *THE COLOR PURPLE*?

A) Tony Morrison

C) Stephen King

B) Alice Walker

D) Margaret Atwood

#31 - WHICH RADIO PERSONALITY WAS POPULAR FOR DISCUSSING SEX AND RELATIONSHIP TOPICS IN THE 1980S?

A) Dr. Ruth Westheimer

C) Roger Christian

B) Dick Biondi

D) Dave Diamond

#32 - WHICH NATION DID THE U.S. FACE IN THE FAMOUS "MIRACLE ON ICE" GAME?

A) China

C) The Soviet Union

B) Canada

D) Great Britain

#33 - WHICH CABLE CHANNEL WAS THE FIRST-EVER 24-HOUR NEWS NETWORK IN THE U.S.?

A) ABC News

C) CBS News

B) CNN

D) CNBC

#34 - WHICH TEAM WON SUPER BOWL XX (1986)?

A) Chicago Bears

C) New England Patriots

B) New York Giants

D) San Francisco 49ers

#35 - WHICH SONG MADE THE EXPRESSION "GAG ME WITH A SPOON" POPULAR?

A) Take On me

C) Don't You

B) Valley Girl

D) Hungry Like the Wolf

#36 - WHEN WAS THE FAMED MOVIE *THE TERMINATOR* RELEASED?

A) 1988

C) 1984

B) 1980

D) 1989

#37 - WHICH OF THESE 1980S FILMS DID NOT INCLUDE HARRISON FORD IN THE CAST?

A) The Empire Strikes Back

C) Blade Runner

B) Indiana Jones and the Raiders of The Lost Ark

D) Midnight Run

#38 - WHICH CHEF POPULARIZED THE FAMOUS BLACKENED FISH RECIPE?

A) Alice Waters

C) Paul Prudhomme

B) Jean Banchet

D) Wolfgang Puck

#39 - WHICH 1987 NOVEL CENTERS ON A RUNAWAY SLAVE HAUNTED BY THE GHOST OF HER MURDERED CHILD, AS SHE EVADES RECAPTURE?

A) The Glory Field

C) Nightjohn

B) Beloved

D) Copper Sun

#40 - WHEN WAS THE CAR AMG HAMMER FIRST RELEASED?

A) 1989

C) 1985

B) 1986

D) 1981

#41 - THE 1980S FASHION STYLE "YUPPIE" WAS AN ACRONYM FOR WHICH PHRASE?

A) Young upwardly-mobile professional

C) You only live once

D) Young and free

B) Young and popular

#42 - WHEN WAS THE BOARD GAME "GUESS WHO?" RELEASED IN THE UNITED STATES?

A) 1979

C) 1987

B) 1989

D) 1982

#43 - WHICH ACTRESS ACCIDENTALLY RELEASED THE CUTOFF SWEATSHIRT FASHION STYLE?

A) Meryl Streep

C) Jennifer Beals

B) Jessica Lange

D) Jane Fonda

#44 - WHO WAS NAMED THE NBA ROOKIE OF THE YEAR ON MAY 16, 1985?

A) Larry Bird

C) Shaquille O'Neal

B) Michael Jordan

D) Scottie Pippen

#45 - WHAT YEAR WAS MICROSOFT WINDOWS FIRST LAUNCHED?

A) 1987

C) 1985

B) 1986

D) 1984

#46 - WHICH 1980S FASHION TREND ORIGINATED FROM PUNK AND ROCK CULTURE?

A) Oversized coats

C) Ripped jeans

B) Spandex

D) Cowboy boots

#47 - WHICH HOUSEHOLD GADGET WAS MARKETED WITH THE CATCHY JINGLE "CLAP ON, CLAP OFF"?

A) Torch

C) The Clapper

B) TV remote

D) Telephone

#48 - WHICH OF THE FOLLOWING ACTORS/ACTRESSES DID NOT STAR IN THE ICONIC 1986 MOVIE *TOP GUN*?

A) Tom Cruise

C) Anthony Edwards

B) Val Kilmer

D) Michael J. Fox

#49 - WHAT FOOD ITEM WAS INTRODUCED TO THE MCDONALD'S MENU IN 1983?

A) Chicken McNuggets

C) Hot Apple Pie

B) Filet-O-Fish

D) Hamburger

#50 - WHO CREATED THE POLLY POCKET TOY?

A) Chris Wiggs

C) Mike Bowling

B) Hasbro Company

D) Howard J. Morrison

#51 - WHEN DID THE UNITED STATES OLYMPIC COMMITTEE VOTE TO BOYCOTT THE SUMMER OLYMPICS IN MOSCOW?

A) 1980

C) 1988

B) 1984

D) 1981

#52 - WHICH VIDEO GAME CHARACTER HAD THE TAGLINE, "THE NEW FEMME FATALE OF THE GAME WORLD"?

A) Lara Croft

C) Ms. Pac-Man

B) Princess Peach

D) Samus Aran

#53 - WHO FATALLY SHOT JOHN LENNON ON DECEMBER 8, 1980?

A) Christopher Scarver

C) John Henry Carpenter

B) Mark David Chapman

D) Charles Manson

#54 - HOW MANY PONIES WERE IN THE ORIGINAL MY LITTLE PONY TOY LINEUP?

A) 4

C) 6

B) 5

D) 7

#55 - WHAT YEAR DID CNN'S *LARRY KING LIVE* FIRST AIR?

A) 1988

C) 1985

B) 1990

D) 1980

#56 - HOW LONG DID THE 1981 BASEBALL PLAYER'S STRIKE LAST?

A) 131 days

C) 232 days

B) 49 days

D) 2 days

#57 - WHO INVENTED THE FIRST ARTIFICIAL HUMAN HEART?

A) Alexander Fleming

C) Jonas Salk

B) Robert Jarvik

D) Frederick Banting

#58 - WHICH 1980S CELEBRITY IS ATTRIBUTED TO MAKING CRIMPED HAIR POPULAR?

A) Cher

C) Barbra Streisand

B) Tina Turner

D) Joan Jett

#59 - HOW MANY SEASONS DID THE 1980s TV SERIES *CHEERS* RUN?

A) 11

C) 8

B) 15

D) 7

#60 - WHAT WAS THE NAME OF HBO'S FIRST ORIGINAL SERIES?

A) Fraggle Rock

C) Video Jukebox

B) Game of Thrones

D) The Succession

#61 - WHO ATTEMPTED TO ASSASSINATE PRESIDENT REAGAN IN 1981?

A) Griselio Torresola

C) John Warnock Hinckley Jr.

B) Oscar Collazo

D) Lee Harvey Oswald

#62 - WHEN DID THE WORLD HEALTH ORGANIZATION DECLARE DECEMBER 1 TO BE WORLD AIDS DAY?

A) 1981

C) 1985

B) 1988

D) 1983

#63 - WHAT NICKNAME WAS GIVEN TO THE DEFENSIVE SYSTEM ADVOCATED BY PRESIDENT RONALD REAGAN?

A) Star Wars

C) Keen Sword

B) Husky

D) Exercise Term System

#64 - WHICH SITCOM POPULARIZED THE WALDORF SALAD?

A) Family Matters

C) Fawlty Towers

B) Who's the Boss

D) Full House

#65 - WHICH 1980S TOY LATER INSPIRED THE MOVIE *JINGLE ALL THE WAY*?

A) The Cabbage Patch Kids

C) Hungry Hungry Hippos

B) Glo Worm

D) Care Bears

#66 - WHICH PHARMACEUTICAL COMPANY INTRODUCED THE WELL-KNOWN ANTIDEPRESSANT PILL PROZAC?

A) Sanofi

C) Johnson & Johnson

B) Bayer

D) Lilly

#67 - WHO WAS THE SECRETARY OF THE TREASURY FROM 1985 TO 1988?

A) William Miller

C) Donald T. Rega

B) James A. Baker, III

D) Nicholas F. Brady

#68 - WHAT YEAR DID THE ANIMATED SERIES *THE SIMPSONS* DEBUT?

A) 1987

C) 1981

B) 1988

D) 1989

#69 - WHICH COMPANY RELEASED THE BOARD GAME "DARK TOWER" IN 1981?

A) Milton Bradley

C) Hot Wheels

B) Hasbro

D) Mattel

#70 - WHAT YEAR WAS THE NICOTINE PATCH INVENTED?

A) 1987

C) 1985

B) 1986

D) 1984

#71 - WHEN DID MTV GO ON AIR FOR THE FIRST TIME?

A) 1981

C) 1983

B) 1982

D) 1984

#72 - WHO CAME UP WITH THE ICONIC 1980S TOY POUND PUPPY?

A) Mike Bowling

C) Howard J. Morrison

B) Steve D'Angelo

D) Muriel Fahrion

#73 - HOW MANY ASTON MARTIN V8 VANTAGE ZAGATO UNITS WERE MADE?

A) 50

C) 52

B) 150

D) 456

#74 - WHICH POPULAR 1980S DISH INSPIRED NATIONAL CHICKEN WING DAY?

A) Chicken nuggets

C) Fiesta chicken

B) Garlic chicken

D) Buffalo wing

#75 – WHICH OF THE FOLLOWING WRITERS GHOST WROTE THE *SWEET VALLEY HIGH* BOOKS?

A) William Gibson

C) Francine Pascal

B) Katherine Heiny

D) Alice Walker

1980s: Answer Key

ANSWER #1: D) GEORGE H. W. BUSH

George H. W. Bush was Ronald Reagan's vice president before becoming president in 1988. He was also a WWII Navy aviator, served in Congress, and led the CIA.

ANSWER #2: B) NBC

The Cosby Show aired on NBC for eight seasons on Thursday nights. It became a top-rated family comedy and focused on the Huxtable family's daily life in Brooklyn.

ANSWER #3: B) SANDRA DAY O'CONNOR

On September 21, 1981, Sandra Day O'Connor was appointed as the first female Supreme Court justice. She served from 1981 to 2006, paving the way for future female justices like Sonia Sotomayor and Ruth Bader Ginsburg.

ANSWER #4: A) Nintendo Game Boy

Released in 1989, the Nintendo Game Boy was the first portable handheld game system with interchangeable cartridges. It featured an 8-bit Z80 processor and 4-channel stereo sound, and included popular games like *Tetris* and *Super Mario Land*.

ANSWER #5: EARVIN JOHNSON

Known as "Magic" from his high school days for his exceptional ball handling, Earvin Johnson Jr. won five NBA championships with the Lakers and three MVP awards.

ANSWER #6: A) THE FLING

Released by Kodak in the 1980s, *The Fling* was a modern disposable camera costing about $6.95. It could take 24 photos and was popular among tourists for its affordability and convenience.

ANSWER #7: B) VERY GOOD

In the '80s, "bad" was used to mean something was actually very good, or even better than good, creating a playful twist on its original meaning.

ANSWER #8: A) TRANSFORMER

Hasbro and Takara released Transformer toys that could transform into robots, cars, guns, and dinosaurs. These toys led to the creation of the *Transformers* movie franchise.

ANSWER #9: C) SPANDEX

Spandex, known for its stretch and shape retention, transformed fashion. It became popular through icons like Jane Fonda and David Lee Roth. The name "spandex" is an anagram of "expands."

ANSWER #10: B) PRINCE

"Purple Rain" solidified Prince as a top songwriter and producer. Originally envisioned as a country song with Stevie Nicks, it evolved into a major hit. The song also inspired a film of the same name, depicting his rise to fame.

ANSWER #11: B) Boombox

The term "boombox" came from its boxy shape and powerful bass. This portable speaker was a key 1980s icon, often carried on shoulders or to outdoor events. As music trends grew, so did the size of boomboxes.

ANSWER #12: B) ESPRESSO MACHINE

Originally invented by Angelo Moriondo in 1884, the espresso machine became popular in European cafes. In the 1980s, advances in production made these machines affordable for American homes.

ANSWER #13: A) MOONWALK

Michael Jackson introduced the Moonwalk, where a dancer glides backward while appearing to walk forward, during his "Billie Jean" performance on May 16, 1983. The move became a global sensation, thanks to the massive TV audience of 47 million.

ANSWER #14: D) BOBBY MCFERRIN

Bobby McFerrin's song "Don't Worry Be Happy" became a feel-good anthem, topping charts worldwide. It won Grammys for Song of the Year, Record of the Year, and Best Male Pop Vocal.

ANSWER #15: A) COUCH POTATO

"Couch potato" was trademarked by cartoonist Robert Armstrong in the '80s. He used the term in cartoons featuring a potato character lounging on a sofa, having first heard it as a joke from a friend.

ANSWER #16: B) CHALLENGER

On January 28, 1986, the Space Shuttle *Challenger* exploded 73 seconds after launch, killing all seven crew members. The disaster was caused by a failed O-ring seal, which malfunctioned in the cold weather, marking the first major shuttle accident.

ANSWER #17: C) SALLY RIDE

Sally Ride became the first American woman in space on June 18, 1983, at age

32. This followed Valentina Tereshkova of the Soviet Union, who was the first woman in space in 1963.

ANSWER #18: D) 1983

The iconic music video, directed by John Landis and featuring a famous zombie dance sequence, was released in December 1983. It became a global hit and won Grammy Awards for Best Video Album in 1984 and Best Video, Long Form in 1985.

ANSWER #19: B) WXRK-FM

The Howard Stern Show, starting in 1985 on WXRK-FM, quickly became a hit, attracting around 20 million listeners with its unique humor and celebrity interviews.

ANSWER #20: B) FORD MUSTANG

The Ford Mustang was the third generation of Ford's iconic muscle car, lasting from 1979 to 1993. It is referred to as the Fox Body since it used the new Fox platform. It was available in 2-door sedan (coupe) and 3-door sedan (hatchback) body styles.

ANSWER #21: C) GENERAL HOSPITAL

Rick Springfield debuted as neurosurgeon Noah Drake on *General Hospital* in 1981. The show's popularity helped propel Springfield to stardom, with his song "Jessie's Girl" hitting number one that year.

ANSWER #22: A) THE CABBAGE PATCH

The *Cabbage Patch* dance involves moving your fists in a circular motion. It gained popularity from Gucci Crew II's song "The Cabbage Patch" and was inspired by the 1980s toy, the Cabbage Patch Kid.

ANSWER #23: D) DENZEL WASHINGTON

Denzel Washington's role in *Carbon Copy* marked his first major Hollywood appearance. The film, an adaptation of the 1970s play *The Engagement Baby*, set the stage for his iconic roles in *The Equalizer*, *Inside Man*, and *Glory*.

ANSWER #24: D) KEN GRIFFEY JR.

Ken Griffey Jr. was renowned for his exceptional hitting skills. The nickname "The Kid" helped distinguish him from his legendary father, Ken Griffey Sr., who was also a celebrated baseball player.

ANSWER #25: D) MARGARET ATWOOD

The Handmaid's Tale depicts a dystopian society where fertile women are forced to bear children for the ruling class. It is renowned for its powerful portrayal of real-world issues.

ANSWER #26: A) J. DASH

In 1986, J. Dash popularized the Wop dance with his hit single "Woppit." The dance features punching the arms up to the opposite side.

ANSWER #27: D) TEARS FOR FEARS

Tears for Fears released "Everybody Wants to Rule the World" on March 15, 1985, from their album *Songs from the Big Chair*. The song topped the Billboard Hot 100 and was a major hit in the UK, reflecting Cold War themes that still resonate today.

ANSWER #28: C) FERRARI F40

The Ferrari F40, unveiled in July 1987, is a highly sought-after supercar with only 1,315 units produced. Supervised by Enzo Ferrari, it remains one of the greatest supercars ever made.

ANSWER #29: B) 6 DAYS

It took John Hughes 6 days to write the script for *Ferris Bueller's Day Off* in the face of the looming writer's strike. Hughes was the mastermind for other popular movies such as *Sixteen Candles* and *The Breakfast Club*.

ANSWER #30: B) ALICE WALKER

John Hughes wrote the script for *Ferris Bueller's Day Off* in just 6 days due to an impending writer's strike. The film is a classic teen comedy set in Shermer, Illinois. Hughes also created *Sixteen Candles* and *The Breakfast Club*.

ANSWER #31: A) DR. RUTH WESTHEIMER

Dr. Ruth Westheimer gained popularity for her frank, humorous, and nonjudgmental approach to discussing intimacy on her late-night radio show, *Sexually Speaking*.

ANSWER #32: C) THE SOVIET UNION

On February 22, 1980, the U.S. hockey team defeated the Soviet Union in what became known as the "Miracle on Ice." Despite being underdogs, the American college players triumphed over the Soviet team.

ANSWER #33: B) CNN

On June 1, 1980, Ted Turner launched CNN, the first channel to offer 24-hour news coverage. This innovation transformed news delivery, offering continuous updates and establishing CNN as a major news source, paving the way for other cable news networks.

ANSWERS #34: A) CHICAGO BEARS

The Chicago Bears made history with back-to-back playoff shutouts and their first Super Bowl win since 1963, scoring a record 46 points. The team featured legends like Jim McMahon, William Perry, and Walter Payton.

ANSWER #35: B) VALLEY GIRL

The phrase "gag me with a spoon," meaning something gross, gained fame through Frank Zappa's 1982 song *Valley Girl*. This song also popularized the distinct dialect of teens in California's San Fernando Valley during the early '80s.

ANSWER #36: C) 1984

The Terminator, released in 1984, is a sci-fi film that launched the *Terminator* franchise. It features a cyborg sent from a dystopian future to kill the mother of a future leader of the human resistance.

ANSWER #37: D) MIDNIGHT RUN

Harrison Ford, a major 1980s Hollywood star known for hits like *The Empire Strikes Back*, was considered for the role of Jack Walsh in *Midnight Run*. However, he did not appear in the film.

ANSWER #38: C) PAUL PRUDHOMME

Chef Paul Prudhomme popularized blackened fish in the early 1980s, leading to a trend in Cajun and Creole fusion dishes. His method of blackening seafood became widely known, almost causing the red drum to face extinction due to high demand.

ANSWER #39: B) BELOVED

Toni Morrison's *Beloved* is acclaimed for its portrayal of slavery's horrors, solidifying her reputation as a leading 20th-century writer and contributing to her Nobel Prize in Literature win in 1993.

ANSWER #40: B) 1986

Released in 1986, the Hammer was a modified Mercedes W124 E-Class with a powerful 5.6L V8 engine. This made it faster than the Lamborghini Countach from 60 to 120 MPH and capable of going from 0 to 60 in just 4.9 seconds.

ANSWER #41: A) YOUNG UPWARDLY-MOBILE PROFESSIONAL

The Yuppie style of the early 1980s included Ralph Lauren skirt suits and Coach bags for women, and pinstripe suits and Rolex watches for men. This look epitomized the professional and affluent lifestyle of young professionals at the time.

ANSWER #42: D) 1982

The board game *Guess Who?* was introduced to the U.S. in 1982 by Hasbro. Originally released in Dutch in 1979 as "Wie is het?", it involves players using yes-or-no questions to guess the face on their opponent's card.

ANSWER #43: C) JENNIFER BEALS

Jennifer Beals popularized the cutoff sweatshirt look in *Flashdance*. The sweatshirt, which had shrunk in the dryer, was altered by Beals to fit her, and its off-the-shoulder style became a fashion trend following the film's success.

ANSWER #44: B) MICHAEL JORDAN

Michael Jordan was a standout at North Carolina, where he was a two-time Player of the Year and made a famous game-winning shot in the NCAA championship. He ranked third in scoring and fourth in steals, eventually becoming one of the greatest players in basketball history.

ANSWER #45: C) 1985

Windows 1.0 was launched on November 20, 1985, marking a significant shift to using a mouse for input. Spearheaded by Bill Gates, it was the beginning of a long series of major Windows updates from Microsoft.

ANSWER #46: C) RIPPED JEANS

Ripped jeans gained popularity in the '80s as a rebellious fashion trend, embodying the counterculture movement. They symbolized nonconformity and evolved into various styles, including acid-washed and patched jeans.

ANSWER #47: C) THE CLAPPER

Introduced in the mid-1980s, The Clapper was the first sound-activated switch for lamps and TVs. It could control up to two appliances and laid the groundwork for modern voice-activated systems like Alexa and Siri.

ANSWER #48: D) MICHAEL J. FOX

Top Gun is about fighter pilots at the Naval Fighter Weapons School in San Diego. The film, praised for its action and depiction of military life, was the highest-grossing domestic film of 1986, earning $176.8 million.

ANSWER #49: A) CHICKEN MCNUGGETS

McDonald's launched Chicken McNuggets in 1983. Initially available in 6-, 9-, and 20-piece servings with various sauces, they quickly became a hit with kids and even gained their own mascot.

ANSWER #50: A) CHRIS WIGGS

Chriss Wiggs developed the toy for his daughter Kate in 1983, featuring a miniature dollhouse. The toy was released to the public in 1989 and quickly gained popularity. Over time, Polly Pocket expanded to include mini castles and mini pet shops.

ANSWER #51: A) 1980

The 1980 Summer Olympics boycott, prompted by the Soviet invasion of Afghanistan, saw 65 nations abstain from the Games. The Soviet Union later led a boycott of the 1984 Los Angeles Olympics in return.

ANSWER #52: C) MS. PAC-MAN

Released in 1982, *Ms. Pac-Man* is a spin-off of the 1980 game *Pac-Man*. It features the same maze-chase gameplay with a new character and improved features.

ANSWER #53: B) MARK DAVID CHAPMAN

Mark David Chapman shot John Lennon outside his residence on Central Park West. Chapman stayed at the scene reading *The Catcher in the Rye* until his arrest. He received a 20-years-to-life sentence.

ANSWER #54: C) 6

The original *My Little Pony* collection included Minty, Butterscotch, Cotton Candy, Blossom, Blue Belle, and Snuzzle. The toy's popularity led to the TV series *My Little Pony: Friendship is Magic*.

ANSWER #55: C) 1985

Larry King Live premiered on June 3, 1985. Hosted by Larry King, the show became a top-rated interview program, featuring presidents, actors, and athletes. It ran for 25 years before its final episode aired in June 2010.

ANSWER #56: B) 49 DAYS

The 1981 MLB strike, which began on July 31, lasted 49 days. It was the longest strike in professional sports at the time, caused by disagreements over free-agent compensation and owners' demands.

ANSWER #57: B) ROBERT JARVIK

The Jarvik 7, developed by Robert Jarvik, was the first artificial heart implanted in a patient on December 2, 1982. Initially meant as a permanent solution, it is now used temporarily for patients awaiting transplants.

ANSWER #58: C) BARBRA STREISAND

Hair crimping was a long procedure where one would take a crimping iron to create zig-zag patterns in their hair. Barbra Streisand's stylist, Geri Cusenza, invented the hairstyle after hours of braiding Streisand's hair.

ANSWER #59: A) 11

Cheers aired from 1982 to 1993. The show, set in a fictional bar, ran for 11 seasons, won 28 Emmy Awards, and attracted 80.4 million viewers for its series finale.

ANSWER #60: A) FRAGGLE ROCK

Fraggle Rock, HBO's first original series, aired from 1983 to 1987. It followed the adventures of five cave-dwelling puppets called Fraggles and helped HBO build its reputation for original storytelling.

ANSWER #61: C) John Warnock Hinckley Jr.

On March 30, 1981, John Hinckley Jr. fired six shots at President Reagan outside the Hilton Hotel in Washington, D.C. Reagan was shot and hospitalized but later recovered. Hinckley was found not guilty by reason of mental illness.

ANSWER #62: B) 1988

World AIDS Day was established by WHO in 1988 to raise awareness of AIDS. By the end of the 1980s, there were at least 100,000 reported cases of AIDS in the U.S. and 400,000 globally.

ANSWER #63: A) STAR WARS

On March 23, 1983, President Reagan proposed the Strategic Defense Initiative, known as "Star Wars," to protect against Soviet nuclear attacks. The name was inspired by the popular space film of the same name.

ANSWER #64: C) FAWLTY TOWERS

The Waldorf Salad was invented in 1893 by Oscar Tschirky at the Waldorf-Astoria Hotel. In the *Fawlty Towers* episode "The Waldorf Salad," the characters' comedic struggle to prepare the dish boosted its popularity.

ANSWER #65: A) THE CABBAGE PATCH KIDS

The Cabbage Patch Kids, created by Xavier Roberts in 1976, gained massive popularity after a 1980 TV appearance. By Christmas 1983, they were a top toy, even inspiring the 1996 film *Jingle All the Way*.

ANSWER #66: D) LILLY

Lilly Pharmaceuticals released Prozac in 1986, marking a major advance in treating clinical depression with fewer side effects than previous drugs. This success contributed to Lilly's growth into a multibillion-dollar company.

ANSWER #67: B) James A. Baker, III

James A. Baker, III, served as Secretary of the Treasury, where he played a key role in passing major tax reforms and promoting American exports. He stepped down in August 1988 to become Chairman of George H. W. Bush's presidential campaign.

ANSWER #68: D) 1989

The Simpsons debuted on December 17, 1989. Created by Matt Groening, it introduced viewers to the Simpson family and became the longest-running American sitcom and animated series, significantly influencing TV and pop culture.

ANSWER #69: A) MILTON BRADLEY

Dark Tower is an infamous collectible game that was released by Milton Bradley Company. One to four players could play. The object of the game is to build an army, collect keys from the Tower, and defeat the evil forces within.

ANSWER #70: D) 1984

Dr. Murray E. Jarvik and one of his students began testing the dermal application of nicotine in 1984. The nicotine patch releases a small, continuous amount of nicotine through the skin.

ANSWER #71: B) 1982

MTV launched on August 1, 1982, with "Video Killed the Radio Star" by The Buggles as its first video. The channel revolutionized music and entertainment, significantly boosting the careers of artists like Prince and Madonna.

ANSWER #72: A) MIKE BOWLING

Mike Bowling created Pound Puppy in 1984, a plush toy with droopy ears and floppy eyes. He sold it to Tonka, where it quickly became a hit with kids due to its various colors and sizes.

ANSWER #73: C) 52

The Aston Martin V8 Zagato, unveiled at the 1986 Geneva Motor Show, had an original production plan for 50 units but ended up with 52. Known for its lightweight and compact design, it became a coveted collector's item.

ANSWER #74: D) BUFFALO WING

In 1977, the mayor of Buffalo, New York, declared July 29 National Chicken Wing Day. Buffalo wings, deep-fried for a crispy exterior and juicy interior, gained widespread popularity in the 1980s, becoming a staple at bars and parties.

ANSWER #75: B) KATHERINE HEINY

In the 1980s, ghostwriting became prevalent for popular teen book series. *Sweet Valley High*, which had 152 titles, employed a team of ghostwriters, including Katherine Heiny, to meet the high demand.

1990s Questions

#1 - WHICH U.S. PRESIDENT WAS THE SECOND TO BE IMPEACHED WHILE IN OFFICE?

A) Bill Clinton

C) Barack Obama

B) George Washington

D) Jimmy Carter

#2 - THE SLANG "TRIPPING" WAS USED TO DESCRIBE WHAT KIND OF PERSON?

A) Crazy

C) Tall

B) Lazy

D) Sick

#3 - WHICH OF THESE FASHION TRENDS WAS POPULARIZED BY TUPAC SHAKUR?

A) Bandanas

C) Bike shorts

B) Neon windbreaker

D) Cut-off tanks

#4 - WHO DESIGNED THE 1997 "TWILIGHT IMPERIUM" BOARD GAME?

A) Milton Bradley

C) Wolfgang Kramer

B) Christian T. Peterson

D) Michael Kiesling

#5 - WHICH ICONIC '90S FILM WAS THE FIRST TO GENERATE ONE BILLION DOLLARS IN REVENUE?

A) Seven

C) Clueless

B) Goodfellas

D) Titanic

#6 - WHICH NBA LEGEND RETIRED IN 1992 AFTER WINNING GOLD AT THE OLYMPICS?

A) Michael Jordan

C) Larry Bird

B) Charles Barkley

D) Magic Johnson

#7 - WHICH '90S DANCE INVOLVED THE ACTION OF PRETENDING TO RUN?

A) Running man

C) The Macarena

B) Tootsee Roll

D) Cabbage Patch

#8 - WHO WROTE THE NOVEL *HARRY POTTER AND THE SORCERER'S STONE*?

A) J. K. Rowling

C) Bret Easton Ellis

B) Francine Pascal

D) Stephen King

#9 - WHAT '90S SLANG WAS USED TO MEAN SORRY?

A) Whatever

C) My bad

B) Buzzkill

D) Dibs

#10 - HOW MANY STRIPES DOES THE FAMOUS ADIDAS TRACKSUIT HAVE?

A) 5

C) 3

B) 6

D) 8

#11 - WHO AMONG THE FOLLOWING WAS NOT A CAST MEMBER OF THE 1994 SHOW *FRIENDS*?

A) Matt LeBlanc

C) Jennifer Lopez

B) Jennifer Aniston

D) Courteney Cox

#12 - WHICH ARTIST PERFORMED THE ICONIC SONG "I WILL ALWAYS LOVE YOU"?

A) Whitney Houston

C) Shakira

B) Beyoncé

D) Lady Gaga

#13 - WHICH POPULAR DANCE OF THE '90S APPEARED AT THE DEMOCRATIC NATIONAL CONVENTION (DNC) IN 1996?

A) The Running Man

C) The Macarena

B) Hammer Dance

D) The Cabbage Patch

#14 - IN WHICH YEAR WAS *THE HOWARD STERN RADIO SHOW* LAUNCHED?

A) 1991

C) 2000

B) 1998

D) 2002

#15 - WHICH FEMALE TENNIS PLAYER WON A GRAND SLAM AT ONLY 17 YEARS OF AGE IN 1999?

A) Venus Williams

C) Coco Gauff

B) Serena Williams

D) Jasmine Paolini

#16 - THE 1995 FILM *BAD BOYS* FEATURED MARTIN LAWRENCE AND WHICH OTHER HOLLYWOOD STAR?

A) Ben Affleck

C) Will Smith

B) Keanu Reeves

D) Morgan Freeman

#17 - WHICH DEVICE WAS LAUNCHED IN 1996 TO REPLACE THE VHS?

A) HDMI

C) DVD player

B) MP3

D) TV Box

#18 - WHICH AMERICAN CAR WAS NICKNAMED "CATFISH"?

A) Ford Mustang SVT Cobra R

C) Ford Taurus SHO

B) Chevrolet Camaro SS

D) Chevrolet Corvette C4 ZR-1

#19 - WHO DID THE VOICE-OVER FOR THE GENIE IN THE 1992 DISNEY FILM *ALADDIN*?

A) Jim Carrey

C) Sinbad

B) Robin Williams

D) Denzel Washington

#20 - WHICH RAP GROUP WAS THE LEGENDARY TUPAC SHAKUR INITIALLY PART OF?

A) Public Enemy

C) Run-D.M.C.

B) Digital Underground

D) Black Star

#21 - WHICH OF THESE WAS NOT A SPIN-OFF OF THE SHOW *LAW AND ORDER*?

A) Law and Order: Special Victims Unit

C) Law and Order: LA

D) Law and Order: Criminal Intent

B) Law and Order: International

#22 - WHICH YEAR DID RAPPER COOLIO RELEASE THE FAMOUS SONG "GANGSTA'S PARADISE"?

A) 1991

C) 1995

B) 1989

D) 2001

#23 WHEN DID THE ATLANTA OLYMPIC BOMBING TAKE PLACE?

A) 1996   C) 1990

B) 2006   D) 1985

#24 - WHICH RADIO PERSONALITY HOSTED *THE HOMETOWN RADIO SHOW* AT WSB FM IN THE "90S?

A) Gary McKee   C) Tom Huges

B) John Lewis   D) Bob Coxe

#25 - THE BACKWARD CAPS FASHION TREND WAS MADE FAMOUS BY WHICH NBA STAR?

A) Gary Payton   C) Kobe Bryant

B) Michael Jordan   D) Scottie Pippen

#26 - WHICH '90s KITCHEN APPLIANCE TOASTED SANDWICHES INTO TRIANGULAR POCKETS?

A) The SuperSnacker   C) The Toaster

B) The Jack LaLanne Juicer   D) Induction Cooktops

#27 - WHICH NEW YORK YANKEES PLAYER WON THE WORLD SERIES MVP AWARD IN 1996, HELPING THE TEAM SECURE THE WIN?

A) Derek Jeter   C) John Wetteland

B) Mariano Rivera   D) Bernie Williams

#28 - WHICH U.S. PRESIDENT LOST TO BILL CLINTON IN THE 1992 PRESIDENTIAL ELECTION?

A) Jimmy Carter

C) Richard Nixon

B) Ronald Reagan

D) George H. W. Bush

#29 - WHICH OF THESE '90s NOVELS WAS NEVER ADAPTED ONTO SCREEN?

A) Fight Club

C) A Game of Thrones

B) Jurassic Park

D) Rabbit at Rest

#30 - WHICH BOXER HANDED MIKE TYSON HIS FIRST BOXING LOSS?

A) Riddick Bowe

C) Buster Douglas

B) Felix Trinidad

D) Evander Holyfield

#31 - WHICH AMERICAN CAR WAS THE FIRST TO EXCEED 400 HORSEPOWER?

A) Ford Mustang SVT Cobra

C) Chevrolet Impala SS

B) Jeep Grand Cherokee (ZJ)

D) Chevrolet Corvette ZR-1 (C4)

#32 - IN WHICH YEAR WAS THE 13 DEAD END DRIVE GAME RELEASED?

A) 1993

C) 1999

B) 1998

D) 1991

#33 - WHAT DANCE WAS ALSO KNOWN AS "CREEP"?

A) Harlem Shake

C) Bart Simpson

B) Humpty Dance

D) The Roger Rabbit

#34 - WHO PLAYED TINA TURNER IN THE FILM *WHAT'S LOVE GOT TO DO WITH IT*?

A) Angela Bassett

C) Halle Berry

B) Whoopi Goldberg

D) Queen Latifah

#35 - WHICH TECH COMPANY WAS LAUNCHED IN 1998?

A) Google

C) Microsoft

B) Apple

D) Tesla

#36 - WHO PLAYED MALCOLM X IN THE 1992 *MALCOLM X* FILM?

A) Will Smith

C) Denzel Washington

B) Morgan Freeman

D) Samuel L. Jackson

#37 - THE FAMOUS "BITE FIGHT" MATCH INVOLVED MIKE TYSON AND WHICH OTHER BOXER?

A) Muhammad Ali

C) Evander Holyfield

B) George Foreman

D) Riddick Bowe

#38 - WHICH YEAR WAS THE "APPLETINI" COCKTAIL CRAFTED?

A) 1990   C) 1994

B) 1996   D) 1988

#39 - WHICH OF THESE FIGHTING COMPANIES WAS ESTABLISHED IN 1993?

A) WWE   C) TKO

B) MMA   D) UFC

#40 - THE 1993 FILM *THE FUGITIVE* STARRED WHICH OF THESE ACTORS?

A) Tom Hanks   C) Bruce Willis

B) Harrison Ford   D) Tom Cruise

#41 - WHICH SHOW WAS KNOWN AS "THE BRADY BUNCH OF THE '90S"?

A) Living Single   C) Charmed

B) Futurama   D) Full House

#42 - WHO INVENTED THE RONCO FOOD DEHYDRATOR?

A) Stephen Poplawski   C) Percy L. Spencer

B) Ron Popeil   D) Moses Coates

#43 - WHICH NFL TEAM LOST FOUR SUPER BOWLS IN A ROW IN THE '90S?

A) Buffalo Bills

C) Minnesota Vikings

B) New York Giants

D) New England Patriots

#44 - WHICH HOLLYWOOD STAR WAS RECOGNIZED AS "AMERICA'S DAD"?

A) Samuel L. Jackson

C) Leonardo DiCaprio

B) Tom Cruise

D) Tom Hanks

#45 - WHICH OF THESE BOOKS WAS WRITTEN BY MICHAEL CRICHTON?

A) Fight Club

C) The Secret History

B) Jurassic Park

D) A Game of Thrones

#46 - WHICH YEAR DID THE FACTUAL EVENTS FROM THE MOVIE *BLACK HAWK DOWN* TAKE PLACE?

A) 1991

C) 1998

B) 1993

D) 2001

#47 - WHO BECAME THE U.S. SECRETARY OF STATE IN 1997?

A) Rex Tillerson

C) John Kerry

B) Madeleine Korbel Albright

D) Condoleeza Rice

#48 - WHICH U.S. WOMEN'S SOCCER PLAYER SCORED THE WINNING PENALTY GOAL TO WIN THE 1999 WORLD CUP?

A) Michelle Akers

C) Carin Gabarra

B) Brandi Chastain

D) Tisha Venturini

#49 - WHICH OF THESE TOYS WAS CREATED BY H. TY WARNER?

A) Giga Pets

C) Beanie Babies

B) Bop it

D) American Girl dolls

#50 - WHICH YEAR WAS THE FIRST EVER TEXT MESSAGE SENT?

A) 1998

C) 1992

B) 1990

D) 1996

#51 - IN WHICH YEAR WAS THE BACKSTREET BOYS FORMED?

A) 1990

C) 1991

B) 1999

D) 1993

#52 - WHO INVENTED THE HAMMER-STRENGTH MACHINES?

A) Keene Dimick

C) Gary Jones

B) Gustav Zander

D) Arthur Jones

#53 - WHO WAS THE REPUBLICAN PARTY NOMINEE FOR THE 1996 PRESIDENTIAL ELECTION?

A) Bob Dole

C) Albert Gore

B) Dan Quayle

D) George W. Bush

#54 - WHICH VEHICLE WAS O.J. SIMPSON RIDING IN DURING THE FAMOUS 1994 SLOW-MOVING CHASE?

A) Cadillac Escalade

C) Ford Bronco

B) Ford Raptor

D) Chevy Tahoe

#55 - WHO DEVELOPED THE "TAE BO" EXERCISE?

A) Ben Bruno

C) Joseph Spinelli

B) Billy Banks

D) Joe Wicks

1990s: Answer Key

ANSWER #1: A) BILL CLINTON

President Clinton was investigated on January 21, 1998, for perjury and obstruction of justice related to an affair with Monica Lewinsky. This led to his impeachment by the House on December 19, 1998.

ANSWER #2: A) CRAZY

The '90s introduced catchy slang, with "tripping" being a popular term to describe someone acting crazy or irrational. This era saw a surge in cool and memorable expressions.

ANSWER #3: A) BANDANAS

The bandana, often worn around the face, neck, or head, gained popularity in the '90s thanks to rapper Tupac Shakur, who styled it as a headband or bow front. It also has religious significance.

ANSWER #4: B) CHRISTIAN T. PETERSON

Twilight Imperium, a board game designed by Christian T. Peterson and produced by Fantasy Flight Games, debuted in 1997 at the Origins Game Fair. Players earn victory points by completing public and secret objectives.

ANSWER #5: D) TITANIC

Titanic (1997), directed by James Cameron, dramatizes the sinking of the RMS Titanic in 1912. Starring Leonardo DiCaprio and Kate Winslet, the film broke box office records and gained immense popularity.

ANSWER #6: C) LARRY BIRD

Larry Bird led the Boston Celtics to three NBA Championships in the 1980s. A 3-time MVP and 12-time All-Star, he retired in 1992 due to back problems, solidifying his place among basketball legends, and cementing a Hall of Fame career.

ANSWER #7: A) RUNNING MAN

The Running Man was a street dance that was famous in the 1980s and 1990s. The dance involved shuffling and sliding steps while imitating a runner. The dance was practiced by some of the best singers and performers such as Janet Jackson and Selena.

ANSWER #8: A) J. K ROWLING

Harry Potter and the Sorcerer's Stone is the first novel by the popular British writer J. K. Rowling. The novel was first published in Britain in 1997 under the title *Harry Potter and the Philosopher's Stone*.

ANSWER #9: C) MY BAD

The slang my bad was a cool '90s slang that was used to mean "you are sorry." This slang originated in the '70s but gained its popularity from the famous '90s film *Clueless*. The term is still used today by many people.

ANSWER #10: C) 3

The origin of tracksuits dates back to the early 1900s with cotton fabric warm-ups. By the 1990s, tracksuits became iconic in hip-hop fashion, with brands like Adidas and Puma popularizing them.

ANSWER #11: C) JENNIFER LOPEZ

The *Friends* sitcom, created by David Crane and Marta Kauffman, aired from

1994 to 2004 on NBC. It followed six New York City friends — Courteney Cox, David Schwimmer, Jennifer Aniston, Lisa Kudrow, Matthew Perry, and Matt LeBlanc.

ANSWER #12: A) WHITNEY HOUSTON

"I Will Always Love You," released on November 2, 1992, became the year's best-selling single and won Grammy Awards in 1994. Whitney Houston is considered one of the greatest female vocalists of all time.

ANSWER #13: C) THE MACARENA

"The Macarena" became a '90s dance sensation from Los del Rio's 1993 hit. It gained major popularity in the U.S. during the 1996 Democratic National Convention, where attendees performed it before the event.

ANSWER #14: B) 1998

The *Howard Stern Radio Show* had its TV debut on August 22, 1998, featuring radio highlights, original content, animated segments, and song parodies. It aired until May 19, 2001.

ANSWER #15: B) SERENA WILLIAMS

Serena Williams was the second African American woman to win a Grand Slam tennis title. At 17 years old, she won the U.S. Open in 1999. She defeated the top-ranked player, Martina Hingis. This victory marked the start of her dominant tennis career.

ANSWER #16: C) WILL SMITH

Bad Boys is an action-comedy film that was released in 1995. It involves two detectives stationed at the Miami Police Department. The film was created by George Gallo and directed by Michael Bay and had several sequels.

ANSWER #17: C) DVD PLAYER

The DVD player, first created by Toshiba in 1996, was released in the U.S. by Sony in 1997. It quickly gained global popularity in the late 1990s.

ANSWER #18: B) CHEVROLET CAMARO SS

The Chevrolet Camaro SS, launched in 1992, is a highly recognizable American car. Known as the "Catfish" for its distinctive front design, it featured a 5.7-liter Pushrod V-8 engine.

ANSWER #19: B) ROBIN WILLIAMS

Robin Williams was an actor and comedian who was widely known for his stand-up routines and diverse film performances. William starred in many films such as voicing the genie in the 1992 animated feature *Aladdin*.

ANSWER #20: B) DIGITAL UNDERGROUND

Tupac Shakur, one of the greatest rappers of all time, joined the hip-hop group Digital Underground in 1990. Known for "The Humpty Dance," the group featured Tupac on two albums before he launched his solo career in 1991.

ANSWER #21: B) LAW AND ORDER: INTERNATIONAL

"Law & Order," which aired from 1990 to 2010 on NBC, is the longest-running law enforcement show in U.S. history. The series, which won a 1997 Emmy for Best Drama, spawned several spin-offs, including *Law & Order: SVU*, *Law & Order: LA*, and *Law & Order: Criminal Intent*.

ANSWER #22: C) 1995

"Gangsta's Paradise" is a rap song by Coolio released on August 1, 1995. The song achieved significant success, becoming the biggest-selling single on the U.S. Billboard charts for that year. It opens with a line from Psalm 23:4.

ANSWER #23: A) 1996

The 1996 Summer Olympics in Atlanta were marred by a bombing in Centennial Park on July 27, which killed one person and injured over 100. The bomber, Eric Rudolph, later received four consecutive life sentences.

ANSWER #24: A) GARY MCKEE

Gary McKee, a radio personality who began his career at 16, joined WQXI AM in 1974 and hosted the popular *Gary McKee Morning Show* for 18 years. He retired from radio in 1999.

ANSWER #25: B) MICHAEL JORDAN

The backward cap trend gained popularity in the 1990s, notably by NBA star Michael Jordan in 1992. Baseball legend Ken Griffey Jr. also helped popularize the style by frequently wearing his cap backward.

ANSWER #26: A) THE SUPERSNACKER

The SuperSnacker was a sandwich toaster that was introduced in the 1990s. This machine toasted sandwiches into triangular pockets. It was a staple in many kitchens in the 1990s due to its ease of use.

ANSWER #27: C) JOHN WETTELAND

John Wetteland was the World Series MVP in 1996, leading the Yankees to their first championship in 18 years. His stellar performance as a closer, including crucial saves, was pivotal to their success.

ANSWER #28: D) GEORGE H. W. BUSH

The 1992 Presidential Election was held on November 3, 1992. President George H. W. Bush sought reelection against Democratic candidate Bill Clinton. Clinton won with 370 electoral votes to Bush's 168.

ANSWER #29: D) RABBIT AT REST

Rabbit at Rest by John Updike was a notable 1990s novel, part of his acclaimed "Rabbit" series. Other key works from the decade include *Fight Club*, *Jurassic Park*, and *A Game of Thrones*, all later adapted into popular films or TV shows.

ANSWER #30: C) BUSTER DOUGLAS

Mike Tyson, considered one of the greatest boxers, faced his first defeat on February 11, 1990, against Buster Douglas. This shocking knockout ended Tyson's unbeaten streak and cost him his heavyweight title.

ANSWER #31: D) CHEVROLET CORVETTE ZR-1 (C4)

The Chevrolet Corvette ZR-1 (C4) was a sleek, modern upgrade from the C3 Stingray. It featured a Lotus-developed engine producing 375 horsepower, later increased to 405 horsepower in 1993, earning it the nickname "Corvette from Hell."

ANSWER #32: A) 1993

13 Dead End Drive is a board game released by Milton Bradley in 1993. Players compete to claim a wealthy older woman's estate by using traps in a mansion-themed board to eliminate other players.

ANSWER #33: C) BART SIMPSON

The Bart Simpson is a 1990s dance inspired by *The Simpsons* character Bart

Simpson. It mimics his skateboarding moves, with one arm positioned behind while facing forward.

ANSWER #34: A) ANGELA BASSETT

What's Love Got to Do with It is a film that was released in June 1993. The film is based on the life of American singer Tina Turner as recorded in her 1986 autobiography.

ANSWER #35: A) GOOGLE

Google, founded by Sergey Brin and Larry Page in 1998, is a leading technology company known for its search engine, online advertising, and software. Today, it's one of the most valuable companies globally.

ANSWER #36: C) DENZEL WASHINGTON

Malcolm X is a 1992 biographical film about the civil rights activist, starring Denzel Washington in the title role. Directed and co-written by Spike Lee, it is based on Malcolm X's 1965 autobiography.

ANSWER #37: C) EVANDER HOLYFIELD

On June 28, 1997, Mike Tyson and Evander Holyfield fought for the WBA Heavyweight Championship. During the match, Tyson bit off a part of Holyfield's ear. Tyson was disqualified and had his boxing license suspended, although it was later reinstated.

ANSWER #38: B) 1996

Appletini, first crafted in 1996, is an apple martini cocktail that is made using apple juice and vodka. The cocktail was initially called Adam's Apple Martini. It was named after the inventor of the drink, Adam.

ANSWER #39: D) UFC

The Ultimate Fighting Championship (UFC) is a mixed martial arts organization founded in 1993. Initially controversial and banned in many states, it was revitalized in 2001 with weight classes and stricter rules.

ANSWER #40: B) HARRISON FORD

The Fugitive is a 1993 film starring Harrison Ford as Dr. Richard Kimble, who is wrongfully convicted of his wife's murder. Directed by Andrew Davis, the film is based on the television series of the same name.

ANSWER #41: D) FULL HOUSE

Full House was a television sitcom show created by Jeff Franklin and ran from September 22, 1987 to May 23, 1995. The show had a total of eight seasons. One of the producers of the show called it "The Brady Bunch of the '90s."

ANSWER #42: B) RON POPEIL

Ron Popeil, founder of Ronco, was a prolific inventor known for creating popular kitchen appliances like the Chop-o-Matic, Dial-O-Matic, Ronco Pocket Fisherman, and the Giant Dehydrator.

ANSWER #43: A) BUFFALO BILLS

The Buffalo Bills were launched in 1967 as a charter club member of the American Football League (AFL). They are known for their passionate fan base. In heartbreaking fashion, the team lost four Super Bowls in a row.

ANSWER #44: D) TOM HANKS

Tom Hanks is an actor known for his dramatic and comedic roles in different films. Hank is mostly referred to as "America's Dad" due to his level of fame and reputation. He is one of the most popular film stars globally.

ANSWER #45: B) JURASSIC PARK

Michael Crichton's *Jurassic Park*, published in 1990, was adapted into a blockbuster film in 1993. The movie achieved massive success, becoming the highest-grossing film at the time.

ANSWER #46: B) 1993

The Battle of Mogadishu, or "Black Hawk Down," occurred on October 3-4, 1993, in Somalia. U.S. forces aimed to capture Somali militia leaders but faced intense resistance, leading to the downing of three Black Hawk helicopters.

ANSWER #47: B) MADELEINE KORBEL ALBRIGHT

Madeleine Korbel Albright served as U.S. Secretary of State from 1997 to 2001, appointed by President Bill Clinton. Prior to this, she was the U.S. Ambassador to the United Nations.

ANSWER #48: B) BRANDI CHASTAIN

The U.S. won the 1999 Women's World Cup by defeating China in a penalty shootout on July 10, 1999. Brandi Chastain secured the victory with the decisive fifth penalty kick.

ANSWER #49: C) BEANIE BABIES

Beanie Babies, created by H. Ty Warner in 1993, became the world's first internet sensation by 1995. Filled with plastic pellets, these toys were often stored as financial investments due to their high resale value.

ANSWER #50: C) 1992

On December 3, 1992, 22-year-old engineer Neil Papworth sent the world's first text message. Using a personal computer and the Vodafone network, Papworth sent "Merry Christmas" to his colleague's phone.

ANSWER #51: D) 1993

The Backstreet Boys, formed in 1993, performed their first show on May 8 at SeaWorld Orlando. They rose after releasing their self-titled album in 1996.

ANSWER #52: C) GARY JONES

The Hammer Strength Machine, invented by Gary Jones in 1989, revolutionized 1990s fitness by mimicking natural body movements, enhancing strength on both sides.

ANSWER #53: A) BOB DOLE

Bob Dole was a U.S. Senator (1969-1996) and the 1996 Republican presidential nominee, losing to President Bill Clinton. Before the Senate, he served in the House of Representatives.

ANSWER #54: C) FORD BRONCO

On June 17, 1994, famous football star O.J. Simpson was wanted by police in connection with the murders of his ex-wife Nicole Brown Simpson and her friend Ron Goldman. Instead of surrendering, Simpson led a 90-minute low-speed chase in his white Ford Bronco, driven by his friend Al Cowlings.

ANSWER #55: B) BILLY BANKS

Tae Bo, a 1990s fitness trend combining martial arts with cardio, was developed by Billy Blanks, a taekwondo and karate expert. It became a pop culture phenomenon during the decade.

2000s to Today Questions

#1 - WHICH OF THE FOLLOWING STATES WAS NOT TARGETED DURING THE SEPTEMBER 11, 2001, TERRORIST ATTACKS?

A) New York City

C) Texas

B) Washington D.C.

D) Pennsylvania

#2 - WHAT IS THE NAME OF THE THIRD PART OF THE LORD OF THE RINGS TRILOGY?

A) The Fellowship of the Ring

B) The Return of the King

B) The Two Towers

D) An Unexpected Journey

#3 - WHAT SLANG WAS COMMONLY USED IN THE 2000S TO DEFINE EXPENSIVE JEWELRY OR ACCESSORIES?

A) Bling bling

C) Diamond

B) Pearls

D) Rock

#4 - WHICH GOLFER BECAME THE FIRST PLAYER TO HOLD ALL FOUR PROFESSIONAL MAJOR CHAMPIONSHIPS AT THE SAME TIME?

A) Tiger Woods

C) Bobby Jones

B) Jack Nicklaus

D) Phil Mickelson

#5 - WHAT YEAR WAS THE IPHONE INTRODUCED?

A) 2001

C) 2006

B) 2012

D) 2007

#6 - HOW MANY STORIES DOES AUTHOR JENNIFER EGAN TELL IN THE NOVEL *A VISIT FROM THE GOON SQUAD*?

A) 7

C) 13

B) 15

D) 9

#7 - WHICH 2020 MINISERIES BOOSTED SALES OF THE CHESS BOARDS?

A) The Queen's Gambit

C) World Wars

B) Jumanji

D) The Games Make

#8 - WHO IS CREDITED FOR CREATING CHAT GPT?

A) Sam Altman   C) John McCarthy

B) Elon Musk   D) Alan Turing

#9 - WHO SANG THE 2008 HIT SONG "SINGLE LADIES"?

A) Adele   C) Beyoncé

B) Taylor Swift   D) Sia

#10 - WHICH CELEBRITY FOUNDED THE WELLNESS AND LIFESTYLE COMPANY GOOP?

A) Gwyneth Paltrow   C) Russell Brand

B) Arianna Huffington   D) Kourtney Kardashian

#11 - WHAT YEAR DID THE *JOE ROGAN EXPERIENCE* FIRST LAUNCH?

A) 2011   C) 2009

B) 2020   D) 2007

#12 - WHO WAS THE SECRETARY OF STATE IN 2014?

A) Antony Blinken   C) Hillary Clinton

B) John Kerry   D) Kamala Harris

#13 - IN WHICH OLYMPIC GAMES DID USAIN BOLT WIN THE 100-METER RACE?

A) Sydney 2000

C) Athens 2004

B) Beijing 2008

D) London 2012

#14 - HOW MANY SUPER BOWLS DID THE NEW ENGLAND PATRIOTS WIN BETWEEN 2000 AND 2020?

A) 3

C) 5

B) 4

D) 6

#15 - WHICH CHEF IS CREDITED WITH CREATING CRONUTS?

A) Isabelle Legeron

C) James Corwell

B) Lena Jüngst

D) Dominique Ansel

#16 - WHICH REPUBLICAN NOMINEE DID BARACK OBAMA BEAT IN THE 2008 PRESIDENTIAL ELECTION?

A) John McCain

C) Mitt Romney

B) Paul Ryan

D) Gary Johnson

#17 - WHICH TELEVISION NETWORK ORIGINALLY AIRED THE ICONIC ANIMATION *AVATAR: THE LAST AIRBENDER*?

A) Cartoon Network

C) Disney Junior

B) Nickelodeon

D) Disney Channel

#18 - WHAT COMPANY WAS FOUNDED BY ELON MUSK TO REVOLUTIONIZE SPACE TECHNOLOGY?

A) NASA   C) Blue Origin

B) SpaceX   D) Space Forge

#19 - WHEN WAS COVID-19 OFFICIALLY DECLARED A PANDEMIC BY THE WORLD HEALTH ORGANIZATION?

A) March 11, 2020   C) January 20, 2020

B) March 1, 2020   D) December 21, 2019

#20 - WHAT YEAR DID THE "GREAT RECESSION" END?

A) 2011   C) 2009

B) 2016   D) 2007

#21 - WHICH OF THE FOLLOWING DID **NOT** LAUNCH FACEBOOK TOGETHER WITH MARK ZUCKERBERG?

A) Andrew McCollum   C) Chris Hughes

B) Dustin Moskovitz   D) Peter Thiel

#22 - WHICH COMPANY WAS THE FIRST PUBLIC COMPANY TO BE WORTH $1 TRILLION?

A) Amazon   C) Microsoft

B) Apple   D) Tesla

#23 - WHAT IS THE NAME OF THE FIRST TESLA CAR?

A) Model S

C) Model Y

B) Model X

D) Tesla Roadster

#24 - WHEN WAS THE PORSCHE 918 SPYDER FIRST SHOWCASED?

A) 2010

C) 2020

B) 2009

D) 2023

#25 - WHICH ARTIST'S DEBUT SINGLE "I KISSED A GIRL" BECAME A WORLDWIDE HIT IN 2008, TOPPING THE CHARTS IN MULTIPLE COUNTRIES?

A) Lady Gaga

C) Katy Perry

B) Rihanna

D) Britney Spears

2000s to Today: Answer Key

ANSWER #1: C) TEXAS

The 9/11 attacks on September 11, 2001, involved four coordinated hijackings by 19 al-Qaeda militants, resulting in nearly 3,000 deaths, with the most fatalities occurring in New York City.

ANSWER #2: C) THE RETURN OF THE KING

The Lord of the Rings film series, based on J.R.R. Tolkien's novel, follows heroes on a quest to save their world. The trilogy includes *The Fellowship of the Ring* (2001), *The Two Towers* (2002), and *The Return of the King* (2003).

ANSWER #3: A) BLING BLING

The term "bling bling" originated from rap music popular in the early 2000s. It was first used to describe expensive jewelry in the 1999 song "Bling Bling," which featured artists from the Cash Money Records label.

ANSWER #4: A) TIGER WOODS

Tiger Woods, considered one of golf's greatest players, dominated the sport in the 1990s and early 2000s. He was the first African American and of Asian descent to win the Masters.

ANSWER #5: D) 2007

On January 9, 2007, Steve Jobs introduced the iPhone, a revolutionary innovation. Its impact was profound. In 2008, Apple launched the App Store, which provided a new platform for third-party apps.

ANSWER #6: C) 13

The novel *A Visit from the Goon Squad* features 13 interconnected chapters, each telling its own story. Acclaimed for its intricate subplots and emotional depth, the 2010 novel earned the Pulitzer Prize for its outstanding narrative.

ANSWER #7: A) THE QUEEN'S GAMBIT

The Queen's Gambit, released on Netflix on October 23, 2020, became the most-watched series in 63 countries. The miniseries follows a young chess prodigy's rise to stardom while battling addiction. Its release boosted chess board sales by about 215%.

ANSWER #8: A) SAM ALTMAN

ChatGPT was developed by OpenAI, co-founded by Sam Altman in 2015. OpenAI aims to create AI that benefits humanity. On November 30, 2022, OpenAI launched ChatGPT, marking a significant milestone in AI development.

ANSWER #9: C) BEYONCÉ

"Single Ladies" was released on October 12, 2008, and is considered one of the best songs of the 2000s. It won Grammy Awards for Song of the Year, Best R&B Song, and Best Female R&B Vocal Performance.

ANSWER #10: A) GWYNETH PALTROW

Gwyneth Paltrow launched Goop as a weekly newsletter and her first book. It grew to 400,000 subscribers, evolving into a multi-platform brand offering wellness services and products.

ANSWER #11: C) 2009

The Joe Rogan Experience debuted on December 24, 2009, hosted by comedian and UFC commentator Joe Rogan. The podcast features long-form conversations with various guests and is one of the most popular in the U.S.

ANSWER #12: B) JOHN KERRY

John Kerry was appointed the 68th U.S. Secretary of State on February 1, 2013. He was the first sitting Senate Foreign Relations Committee Chairman to become Secretary of State in over a century.

ANSWER #13: B) BEIJING 2008

Usain Bolt set a record at the 2008 Olympics, running 100 meters in 9.58 seconds. His record still stands. In 2009, he further cemented his status as the "Fastest Man Alive" at the World Championships.

ANSWER #14: D) 6

Between 2000 and 2020, the New England Patriots won six Super Bowls, with victories in the 2001, 2003, 2004, 2014, 2016, and 2018 seasons. This achievement solidified their status as one of the NFL's greatest dynasties.

ANSWER #15: D) DOMINIQUE ANSEL

Pastry chef Dominique Ansel is credited with creating cronuts at his bakery in New York in 2013. Cronuts resemble a doughnut filled with flavored cream with a croissant-like dough. The dessert became an instant sensation.

ANSWER #16: A) JOHN MCCAIN

On November 4, 2008, Barack Obama was elected the 44th U.S. President, making history as the first African American to hold the office. He defeated John McCain with 365 electoral votes to McCain's 173.

ANSWER #17: B) NICKELODEON

Avatar: The Last Airbender follows four nations at war with each other, with the Avatar being able to restore peace. The show ran from 2005 to 2008 on Nickelodeon, with Dante DiMartino and Bryan Konietzko as co-creators.

ANSWER #18: B) SPACE X

Founded in 2002 by Elon Musk, SpaceX revolutionized space travel. In 2010, it became the first private company to launch a spacecraft into orbit and safely return it to Earth.

ANSWER #19: A) MARCH 11, 2020

COVID-19 was first reported on December 31, 2019, in Wuhan, China. On March 11, 2020, after cases surpassed 100,000, the World Health Organization declared it a global pandemic.

ANSWER #20: C) 2009

The economic downturn spanned from December 2007 to June 2009. The Obama administration invested over $1 trillion in Treasury bonds and $80 billion in Chrysler and General Motors. By Q3 2009, GDP turned positive.

ANSWER #21: D) Peter Thiel

While in his second year at Harvard, Mark Zuckerberg developed the software called Facemash. Andrew McCollum, Dustin Moskovitz, and Chris Hughes also contributed to its development. This software developed into Facebook.

ANSWER #22: B) APPLE

Apple became a leader in the tech industry, reaching a $1 trillion valuation in mid-2018 and $2 trillion by August 2020. The 21st century has seen companies like Microsoft, Apple, Amazon, and Google dominate.

ANSWER #23: D) TESLA ROADSTER

Unveiled in 2006, the first Tesla car, based on the Lotus Elise, boasted over 200 miles of range. On sale from 2008 to 2012, it was among the first to prove that electric vehicles could capture the interest of car enthusiasts.

ANSWER #24: A) 2010

The Porsche 918, designed by Michael Mauer, debuted at the 2010 Geneva Motor Show. Production began in 2013 with a base price of $845,000 and ended in mid-2015, making it a collector's item.

ANSWER #25: C) KATY PERRY

Katy Perry's 2008 debut single "I Kissed a Girl" became a global hit, topping charts in over 20 countries. The song's catchy tune and provocative lyrics launched her into pop stardom.

A Parting Gift

As a way of saying thank you for your purchase, we're offering four FREE downloads that are exclusive to our book readers!

Here's what you'll get:

1. Boomer Brain Teasers: 75 (new) Trivia Questions Spanning the '60s, '70s, '80s, and '90s

2. The Golden Years Word Find: 20 Nostalgic Word Searches for Seniors

3. Heartwarming Tales: 20 Uplifting Short Stories for Seniors

4. The Retirement Movie Marathon: 20 Feel-Good Movies All Seniors Will Love

With all this, you'll have plenty of fun games and activities to feel that nostalgia and keep your mind sharp through the decades!

To download your bonuses, you can go to MonroeMethod.com/trivia-bonus or scan the QR code below:

Can You Do Us a Favor?

Thanks for checking out our trivia book!

We hope you had a ton of fun along the way.

Might you take 60 seconds and write a quick blurb about this book on Amazon?

Reviews are the best way for independent authors (like us) to get noticed, sell more books, and spread our message to as many people as possible. We also read every review and use the feedback to write future revisions—and also future books.

Thank you—we really appreciate your support.

About the Author

Garrett Monroe is a pen name for a team of writers with expertise in retirement planning, puzzle books, and estate planning. These writers have come together to produce a series of fun brain-boosting puzzle books to help you stay sharp and enjoy your golden years!

Made in the USA
Las Vegas, NV
28 December 2024

15507701R00096